MW01137146

Return to Chiloé

Treasures from the Island

DIANA DELACRUZ

Heart Ally Books, LLC
Camano Island, Washington

Bible quotations used throughout with permission and noted according to the following:
Scripture quotations designated (KJV) from The Authorized (King James) Version. Rights in the Authorized Version in the United Kingdom are vested in the Crown. Reproduced by permission of the Crown's patentee, Cambridge University Press
Scripture quotations taken from the (NASB®) New American Standard Bible®, Copyright © 1960, 1971, 1977, 1995, 2020 by The Lockman Foundation. Used by permission. All rights reserved. www.lockman.org
Scripture quotations designated (MSG) from THE MESSAGE. Copyright © by Eugene H. Peterson 1993, 2002, 2005, 2018. Used by permission of NavPress. All rights reserved. Represented by Tyndale House Publishers, Inc.
Scripture designated (NKJV) taken from the New King James Version®. Copyright © 1982 by Thomas Nelson. Used by permission. All rights reserved.
Scripture quotations designated (ESV) are from the ESV® Bible (The Holy Bible, English Standard Version®), copyright © 2001 by Crossway Bibles, a publishing ministry of Good News Publishers. Used by permission. All rights reserved.

Published by:
Heart Ally Books, LLC
26910 92nd Ave NW C5-406, Stanwood, WA 98292
Published on Camano Island, WA, USA
www.heartallybooks.com

ISBN-13: 978-1-63107-051-8 (epub)
ISBN-13: 978-1-63107-050-1 (paperback)
Library of Congress Cataloging-in-Publication Data

Names: Delacruz, Diana, 1958- author.
Title: Return to Chiloé : treasures from the island / Diana Delacruz.
Description: Camano Island, Washington : Heart Ally Books, LLC, [2023] | Series: Seaglass sagas | Summary: "A life-changing trek from memories of the past to hope for the future... Join author Diana Delacruz on a nostalgic six-day return journey to her former home in southern Chile, a little-known island shrouded in mist and mystery that shifted her life experience in subtle yet significant ways. In this travel memoir complemented by meditations on local mythology, Diana chases and checks off adventures on her Chiloé Islands bucket list: sleep in a palafito with an ocean view, eat clambake-in-a-pot, tour heritage architecture, discover hidden hamlets, savor the sunset over the Pacific. Along the way, questions surge to challenge her: Did our work here all those years ago matter? How can I harmonize my love for this land and its people with the desperate need for transformation we all share? Can I reach and touch eternity amid the harsh realities of life here? Diana uncovers gems of bright sea glass among the darkness of generations steeped in myths and legends. Surprises sweep her up as God's true story, the only remedy for false narratives, renews her faith. Her prayer-and ours-becomes, God, let me see what matters. Help me sort treasure from trash, crystals from clamshells"-- Provided by publisher.
Identifiers: LCCN 2022052060 (print) | LCCN 2022052061 (ebook) | ISBN 9781631070501 (paperback) | ISBN 9781631070518 (epub)
Subjects: LCSH: Delacruz, Diana, 1958---Religion. | Delacruz, Diana, 1958---Travel--Chile. | Hispanic American authors--Religious life. | Christian authors--Chile--Biography. | Chiloé Island (Chile)--Description and travel.
Classification: LCC BV4596.A85 D45 2023 (print) | LCC BV4596.A85 (ebook) | DDC 241/.042092 [B]--dc23/eng/20230126
LC record available at https://lccn.loc.gov/2022052060
LC ebook record available at https://lccn.loc.gov/2022052061

1 2 3 4 5 6 7 8 9 10

In memory of
William and Jessie Strong,
who first caught the vision for the Chiloé Islands;
George and Letty Black,
who passed the torch on to me;
and my missionary colleagues and mothers,
Sadie Minnis of Belfast, Northern Ireland
and Helen Prado of Los Angeles, California—
You're my heroes!

Contents

Going Home

Until we reach our final destination in heaven, a world Christian never feels completely at home. You might say it's part of the price we pay for being able to make ourselves a home anywhere.

While I haven't lived everywhere, I aim to think globally about God's purposes on Earth and learn joy and confidence wherever He takes me in the world.

That, of course, isn't the same as clinging to the world or belonging to the world. We don't. In fact, just the opposite. Collecting treasures from around the globe, I recognize I'm on a continuing journey of transformation from glory to glory on my way to glory.

Grasping the worldview of the apostle Paul will transform the outlook on our journey: *"Everywhere and in all things, I am instructed both to be full and to be hungry"* (Phil. 4:12, KJV). The world Christian is destined to feel forever homesick, yet always quite at home. Longing, yet satisfied. Never far from home, never yet arrived. No matter where I am, my heart is here and also there.

In my young adult novel, *Destiny at Dolphin Bay*, the character Melissa Travis wrestles with a school essay entitled

"What I Learned in Chile." I call this memoir my personal version of her assignment. As I pick up sea glass jewels in my travels, I also gather nuggets of wisdom and life lessons to add to my spiritual treasure trove.

Welcome to the mystical Archipelago of Chiloé, a tiny niche of the globe where I lived with my husband and three small daughters for eight years through the decade of the 1980's. *Where in the world is Chiloé?* you may well ask. The long, narrow Republic of Chile showcases a vast variety of landscapes and climates along its 4500 kilometers of coastline. Just off the mainland around the 43rd parallel lies the island group called Chiloé.

To say these are South Pacific islands would be perfectly correct yet totally misleading. Think pines, not palms. Frigid, rockbound coasts, not warm sandy beaches. And rain thirteen months a year, or eight days a week—whichever adds up to more.

What's so special about this singular place I once called home? At that long-ago time in that far-away place—during a period of socio-political upheaval in the country, amid a breathless ministry pace and the nonstop activity of a young family—I learned, I'm sure, a great deal that I can't recall now. I seldom paused long enough then to reflect or to search for buried treasure and hidden gems in this "last corner of the earth."

So I have to go back. Though not all my Seaglass Books are set in the islands, they are rooted and grown out of Chiloé. I feel the need to retrace my steps on the gravel shores, breathe the bracing salt air, and re-encounter my first love for this land and its peculiar people.

My original teenage character, Melissa, traveled to Chiloé as an American visitor, unaware, like me and perhaps many of my readers, of Chile's bumpy past. Now I'm returning as Diana, the missionary writer fast hurtling through middle age and familiar with the modern Chilean scene.

Even so, I'm still truly Melissa, discovering unexpected pearls in an isolated oyster of an island, finding parables in this fabled chest of misty memory and magic.

What stands out on my return to Chiloé? What do I dig up and re-connect with here? I invite you to get out your *mate* cup and come along with me on an adventure to another world, a world I love. I didn't grow up here, and I certainly wasn't born here. Maybe it was never *my* world, but once…it was my home.

Here I'll touch again and weave together the threads of that long-ago life, so full and fantastic, so lush and lonely that it gives me shivers still. What am I searching for? Stories that matter.

Back to Chiloé

If you've read my novel *Destiny at Dolphin Bay*, you'll recognize the story universe of the Chiloé Islands. As the character Melissa connected with island life, she unpredictably fell in love with Chiloé and its people, almost against her will. I learned to love them the same way.

So today I'm launching us into an exploration of Chile's remarkable southern islands, at the crack-off of the continent and the cusp of northwestern Patagonia. Like Melissa later in the series (Desert Island Diaries), I long to go back to Chiloé after a long absence.

Oh, not to live. "We" Chileans are people of countless contradictions, but I admit I'm now spoiled in Chile's sunny central valley by blue skies, export-quality fruit, and beaches with, ahem, actual *sand* (as opposed to stones and gravel). I enjoy summer clothes and sandals, salad season, and sizzling Christmases. And oh yeah, the malls of Santiago.

But for a visit, no spot on earth charms the heart like those picturesque islands. In the first decade after we moved north in 1992, we traveled back to Chiloé regularly. At least, often enough to maintain a feel for the changes, teach the occasional class, watch the neighbor kids grow up, and check the old saltbox house hadn't fallen down yet. We kept caught up with the old friends and introduced new ones to our passion for the place.

Not anymore, though. We haven't been back to Chiloé since we christened the latest "fishers-of-men" launch, *Mensajero (Messenger) III*, with our muddy footprints. And that's only once in the fifteen years since our friends Zoe and Tito's* marine wedding where we drove the newlyweds around town for their post-ceremony getaway (a Chilean tradition!) and the reception began so late our middle daughter fell asleep over the abalone appetizers. Never mind making it to the midnight cake cutting.

Perhaps we dreaded going back to Chiloé after our old home burned down. We'd never bid it a proper good-bye, and somehow that was okay. It still felt like home. As if we'd never really left, only gone on a long furlough.

Jumping off the Continent

But now… Things are changing a lot, and we haven't visited in more than ten years. In the midst of writing *The Sea-Silk Banner*, the finale of Melissa's story, I sense the need of a refresher. A new tale I call *Hope Chest*, about Angélica, a native Chilote girl coming of age at a crucial moment in Chilean history, has also been spinning in my imagination.

We have a significant wedding anniversary approaching. A more perfect opportunity won't likely ever present itself. I want to go, *but* I've spent the past four months struggling with health issues and under-functioning. I'm afraid to take the leap and end up miserable the entire trip.

However, my husband books the plane tickets and car rental and encourages me to plan our six days of relaxation and research. (Division of labor there.) I do so, still wondering how it will all turn out.

> *"Arise, my darling… and come along!"*
> −Song of Solomon 2:14 (NASB)

Then, a miracle: One morning, just a week or two before the trip back to Chiloé, I wake up with all pain vanished. We pack in high anticipation and fly out of the capital of Santiago on an early morning flight.

…And into the port of Puerto Montt, last mainland city. There's an airport on Grand Chiloé now, located between Castro and Dalcahue, the perfect hub for our touring adventure. But practical considerations have won out as we earlier weighed the cost of rentals out of the mainland compared with the small island airport. Besides, we'll get more of a glimpse of the countryside by driving and a ferry ride to boot.

We've always liked Puerto Montt anyway. Our youngest daughter was born during a ferocious winter tempest here. Once again, I look for the statues of the original German colonists that someone told us mark this "jumping-off point" to Chiloé. I still can't locate them, but I've featured those immigrant families in *Legacy of the Linnebrink Light.*

Neither do we find the string of colorful concrete grottos, choked with smoking candles, that used to hedge a couple of alleys leading to the highway.

Crossing the Channel

But Puerto Montt's no longer the quaint little city, hugging multiple hills, that we knew before. It's mushroomed into a sprawling, cosmopolitan megalopolis. We almost get lost winding out of there toward Pargua and the ferry dock. "Terminal," it never was—and still isn't.

Officially it's spring, albeit barely, and (we know all too well) early spring in Chiloé is basically still winter. Yet we pride ourselves on being good Chilotes who won't melt in the rain. We board the ferry under typical gray clouds and drizzle and feel right at home.

Despite traversing the Chacao Channel countless times before, we climb out of our rental car to explore. After all, several of my story characters meet on such a voyage. Melissa arrives for the first time in Chiloé via bus and ferry. And years later, *The Seagull Operation* conducts her on a perilous mission via this crossing. I want to experience again the whipping wind, the stinging cold edged with ice, the odors of brine and diesel.

The Chiloé ferries, run by two main companies, often boast names from Chilote mythology: *La Pincoya, El Trauco,* etc. This one resembles dozens of others we've traveled on over the years.

That is, until we discover the addition of a novel passenger "lounge." This long narrow cabin displays a row of brightly painted wooden tables anchored to the deck and beadboard walls papered with posters advertising Chilote tourism: The gastronomic delights, the new national parks, the heritage-church restoration program. If the place seems a little garish and grimy, hey, in the old days, you'd have been hard pressed to find a toilet aboard.

Hitting the Highlights

We don't notice the differences immediately upon docking on Chiloé. The beacon, the pier, the Coast Guard office…all appear the same as always. Maybe the building has been enlarged and renovated, even rebuilt? And thanks to Sernatur [the government tourism service], a lovely new BIENVENIDOS A CHILOÉ sign scrolls over the entrance to the island.

"Your life is a journey you must travel with a deep consciousness of God…" –I Peter 1:18 (MSG)

It takes over an hour to drive from the ferry to the small city of Castro. Like horses galloping for the barn, we race by Ancud, colonial capital of the archipelago and Castro's rival. We'll plan to stop on our return, but for us today, back to Chiloé means back to El Sacho.

And we're almost late for lunch. We roll into town, barely glancing at the burgeoning growth and transformations, and beeline for Thompson Street. Hoping and praying that our favorite restaurant still exists.

It does! Near the end of a quiet side street, Restaurant El Sacho still nestles in its cloak of cedar shingles, this year's colors hydrangea blue with lemon yellow trim. The antique stone anchor that the rustic café takes its name from still swings overhead.

We push open the double French doors. So much remains the same, true to iconic Chilote architect Edward Rojas's original design: The glistening waxed wood floors, the lime linens and eclectic assortment of chairs, the polished slab counter beneath huge, mullioned windows painted to resemble stained-glass scenes of Chilote life and legends. The Bosca wood stove blazes in the corner near the wooden staircase, and...

Catching Up

As we mount the stairs to the main room, we see our favorite waitress. "Sara!"*

Unbelievably, she is still here. She recognizes us in an instant, abandons her tray on a buffet, and runs to hug and kiss us. Like the memories of a dream, we reminisce about...

...our first visit to El Sacho, for an anniversary dinner decades ago, when we ordered *apio* at Sara's suggestion—without a clue we'd get celery!

...the years of shopping-day lunches and the many times the Sacho staff hurried the *menú del día* so we could get our kids to school on time.

...the kids ordering fried eggs and steamed mussels instead of something more interesting from an adult point of view; their regular visits to the kitchen to say hi to the grandmotherly cook; the mural of napkin notes and sketches.

...the ivy that poked its way inside and crept along until it blanketed the wall beside "our" window table. "Gone now." Sara shrugs. "It was taking over."

...the saffron-haired hostess, equally comfortable in her clicking high heels and battered pickup, always greeting us warmly. "Ah, *la dueña*... Señora Inés* passed away last year," Sara explains. "But the girls and I pooled our savings and bought the business. We're keeping it going."

She dashes down to find the two other former waitresses who now co-own El Sacho. They, too, traipse upstairs to smile and welcome us back to Chiloé and our old stomping grounds, where we'd all once been young and new at our work.

After the reunion, we are seated in the familiar, light-filled dining room. The same pine walls, carved wood panels, and woven reed figurines. Updated with sparkling white trim, sapphire tablecloths, and a collection of baskets and wicker-clad bottles. I miss the trailing ivy, though.

Coming Home

Our meal at El Sacho won't soon be forgotten. I have *locos mayo*, cold abalone with lemon and mayo, and *congrio* (conger eel) fish and chips. My husband, of course, sticks with his old faithful *lomo a lo pobre*, "poor man's" steak and fries topped with easy-over eggs and caramelized onions. We eat ever so leisurely, watching the rain drip off the zinc roofs outside and the fishing launches huddled in the harbor below.

This is the setting, removed to a nearby village in my story world, where Captain Serrano invites the students from the Desertores island group to celebrate their big music festival win (in *Legacy of the Linnebrink Light*). Here, down the road of time, Melissa teaches Bible classes and befriends a solitary islander. It's where one day she'll plan her wedding.

Mingled with the nostalgia this afternoon at Restaurant El Sacho, I remember why I've come back to Chiloé. I recall the many things I love about the islands and the south of Chile. The soft and steady melody of falling rain, the lonesome screech of gulls, the crackling fires, steamy windows and cuddly sweaters. I realize I love warm wood so much better than cold bricks and tile. And I prefer the aroma of mint sprigs to tea bags.

When we tell the Sacho ladies it's my husband's birthday, they treat us to the most exquisite cake I've ever eaten. Raspberry meringue as smooth as silk. We savor every bite.

An awesome beginning to our trip back to Chiloé.

"What if we still ride on, we two, with life forever old yet new, Changed not in kind but in degree, the instant made eternity?"
–Robert Browning, *The Last Ride Together*

*Names have been changed.

Legends of Chiloé

Many, *many* years ago, as a young wife and mother newly settled into the so-called godforsaken Islands of Chiloé, I encountered a cultural bubble where life plodded on much as it had for centuries. Planting, harvesting, tides, and weather ruled life, not technology and toys. Sí, a salmon boom flourished, big business. But so did seaweed soup, ox carts, battered fishing craft, and bizarre superstitions.

One visitor to this realm of coastal hamlets and pastoral landscapes suggested it resembles the Shire of *Lord of the Rings* fame. Sounds enchanting, and truly it is. Yet like Tolkien's Middle Earth, it's deeply flawed. Fallen, the peace and order an illusion. For, what happens to religion without the bliss of God, to beauty without the restraint of virtue? Indeed, it becomes as bleak as the kingdom of Rohan, perilously close to the Black Lands, under the specter of death.

The archipelago also has a unique epic mythology, including their own version of the worldwide flood. Since I've always enjoyed folklore and fairy tales, starting with Cinderella as a child and moving onto Greek mythology in high school, the storyteller in me was intrigued.

*"Everything you look at can become a fairy tale, and you
can get a story from everything you touch."*
–Hans Christian Andersen

In my understanding, almost all legends are rooted at least partly in fact. They often attempt to account for the uncontrollable forces of nature or the otherwise inexplicable. Take the Chilote origins myth, for example, which recounts an epic battle between two serpent-spirits. Hmm, wonder where they got that from?

Some of the tales are admittedly grim. Islanders keep long memories and dark secrets. The ancestors of my neighbors spun yarns to explain their insulated world, to generate fertility in earth and seas, and (forgive my blunt appraisal) to cover up robbery, rape, abuse, and adultery.

Do they believe their own stories? Debatable, these days. Even the most uneducated will laugh as they tell you. Yet, in a place where the winds of change blow rarely, the old tales do provide a convenient barrier to new ideas.

Once Upon a Time...

Still, I admire their embrace of a distinctive cultural heritage... except where it justifies entrenched sins more than it preserves traditional pastimes. And I'm all for the fun of a story...unless it's a story that culminates in death or shackles people in fear and darkness and mental stagnation.

As the character Nicolás Serrano declares in *Destiny at Dolphin Bay*: *"We've been redeemed from this futile way of life..."* (I Pet. 1:18, NASB paraphrase). Years before, his mother, Angélica De la Cruz, lamented that *"instead of sweeping the*

*cobwebs from our gloomy corners...we cowered in the shadows,
mired in the sludge of an occult underbelly."* She acknowledged
growing up *"on the fringes of modern society, at the border of
turmoil and terror."*

What do they mean?

Much of Chiloé's mythology relates to the darkly
paranormal and esoteric. A complex web of witchcraft lore
figures prominently in the tales. For some, a chasm divides
magic from reality; for others, it is but a hairline crack, a
feather fracture, a breath. We can only speculate about the
reality behind the myths.

But whatever the background of truth, these stories frequently underline a thirst for power and revenge and a craving
for health-wealth-and-happiness. Along with the failure of
religion to meet people's deep and genuine needs. I perceive a
pattern of decidedly less-than-upright characters determined
to seize their dreams and desires through violence and/or
deceit.

Do the Chilotes believe their own mythology?

As I say, I don't know about the majority today. But did they
believe as recently as fifty years ago, the time setting of *Hope
Chest*, the future project I'm nurturing about Angie De la
Cruz and her mother, Luisa? On this trip, I'm "investigating"
a rumor that Doña Luisa's grandmother used to turn herself
into a crow to carry messages for a local coven. (Mulling over
the plot possibilities of such a far-fetched claim, in other
words.)

Among other themes in *Hope Chest*, I want to explore the
mist-shrouded path from bizarre reality to legend and myth:

The relationship between Chiloé's fantastical mythology, the very real phenomenon of evil in the world, and a Christian worldview.

Whatever beliefs people held then, most were based on ancient superstition and fear-fueled imagination. Maybe hallucinations from over-indulging in *chicha* or *licor de oro*.

Much Chilote folklore reads like a horror novel or psychological thriller. To begin, we must trace this history mystery back to the mid-1700's, under Spanish colonial oppression. In the inhospitable climate of the Chiloé Archipelago—even more isolated, neglected, and fiercely independent than the rest of southern Chile—a shadowy group of indigenous people formed an underground society known as the Righteous Province or *Los Mayores* (the Majority, or the Elders). So "they" say.

Secrets of the "Unrighteous" Province

Their original "purpose statement," apparently, was to oppose the Spanish elite and provide an alternative regime offering justice for the natives. A prototype of resistance organization. Even during Chile's War for Independence, the Chilotes held out against the new republican government until 1826, eight years after the remainder of the country.

On the bottom line, they meant to maintain their secret knowledge and culture and to dominate the power structure of their island province. By whatever means necessary.

Their members? At a series of so-called witch trials in 1880, the primary accused, a 70-year-old farmer, Mateo Coñuecar, described the Righteous Province as a sect of *brujos* (warlocks). Self-proclaimed kings and viceroys headed their convoluted hierarchy.

Almost all these servants of the Evil One were said to be men. Women usually participated only by serving as *voladoras* (flying messengers/spies disguised as birds) or as healers, skilled in herbal medicine. However, it's those women they usually depict as beak-nosed hags in streaming cloaks.

In Hispanic culture, many concepts of witchcraft are based on the Spanish master Goya's ghoulish paintings. (A topic for another day, but why do the old stories and art denigrate women like that, especially *aging* women?)

But the truth is, the tufts of gray hair under a kerchief and the bent back beneath a black shawl describe an average elderly woman in Chiloé. She could be somebody's grandmother or any poor island widow today. Or almost any matron over thirty in Victorian-era Chile.

Most *brujos* were indigenous people or *mestizos*, for whites of any ethnic descent were seldom trusted. With the elaborate series of brutal initiation rites to pass, not just anyone could gain admittance to the council of Elders anyway.

Their practices? The Righteous Province combined in a sinister way those European pseudo-Christian ideas about witchcraft, imported by the Spaniards, with the beliefs and traditions of the local inhabitants of Chiloé.

According to Coñuecar's testimony, the covens met in caves throughout the islands. Their main base was located in a vast cavern on the sheltered east coast outside the village of Quicaví. A pair of monsters, the Chivato and the Invunche, guarded its concealed entrance. These were once human babies, kidnapped and horribly, deliberately, deformed in infancy.

From Deception to Devilry

Most of the Chilote population dreaded and respected the members of the Righteous Province because of what they considered supernatural powers. The warlocks could lance curses, poison animals or people, and inflict deep slashes, via the evil eye or even from a distance. Terrifying enemies!

Later, however, though tangled with the trappings of magic and mystery, the Righteous Province mostly plotted to fleece and otherwise control their poorer neighbors. Threatened with dead sheep or crops destroyed by sorcery, the "clean" (non-witch) villagers paid an annual "tribute" that the ruling council demanded.

Clearly, the Righteous Province had mutated into a mafia of sorts, running a complex undercover protection racket in the islands and fostering fear for the purpose of manipulation and material gain.

While fairy tales are entertaining, a darker reality often skulks beneath the old-fashioned charm. For these men and women who flirted with demonic forces, the mythology represented a delusion that allowed them to literally get away with murder, extortion, theft—and worse.

Behind closed doors, in clandestine places like Quicaví, they invented the Invunche (I imagine a sort of cave troll) as they molested and exploited defenseless children. They turned their women into *voladoras* and *fiuras*, tough, ignorant creatures whose only role was barefoot, back-breaking work. Teenage pregnancies (and often rape and incest) were blamed on a lecherous forest goblin, the Trauco. And the Pincoya, a fertility mermaid-goddess, received praise for the ill-gotten profits of fishing violations.

Even the legendary phantom ship *Caleuche*, highlighted in *Destiny at Dolphin Bay*, not only explained shipwrecks but also excused strange disappearances and lucrative contraband cargoes, the source of many warlocks' wealth.

Unhappily Ever After...

It all begs the breathless question: How did they ever get away with it?

On the one hand lies bondage to the threat of retribution, of course. On the other, I believe pride in their culture comes into play. In the syncretistic mix of paganism and medieval Christianity that was—and often still is—Chiloé, even ordinary islanders enjoyed bragging rights to this secret order and the sense of belonging to an exclusive in-group.

The Righteous Province, while unrighteous as the devil himself, advocated many popular policies: Anti-outsider, anti-government, anti-law. Some of this volatile, festering bitterness has struck ready kindling and set ablaze the movement of indigenous violence raging in pockets of southern Chile in the present day.

Some fine points of these old stories carry hints of the gospel of Christ. Ways that we can shift the focus to the Real Story. Over time, I've begun to catch a glimpse, decipher a narrative of hope glimmering through the leaden clouds. We don't believe in monsters and myths; we believe the Truth behind the myths.

Don't we all have a transcendent desire to see ourselves as special? What are the superhero movies about, if not that?

Don't we long to discover a source of joy, delight, satisfaction? To belong to a close-knit community and participate in a vision that's bigger than ourselves?

But we *can* find it all in our Lord Jesus Christ. His kingdom, ruled by an all-powerful Prince, encompasses a community of the truly "counted-righteous," where peace and pleasure do indeed last forever.

New Legends of Chiloé

How did a *gringa* like me, from a little town in Maine, ever end up in this remote island in southern Chile? Poised on the brink of stirring times, I had little idea at first of living through history—let alone of altering it. I set about experiencing Chiloé and its idiosyncratic way of life and learning tidbits from farming to fishing, medicine to mythology. Flora and fauna. Herbal lore and tidal shores, crafts and culture. I found it fascinating—and formidable.

And like the character Melissa, I told Bible stories. Week after week, I cracked open the doors of minds and imaginations to let the Light into the Islands of Chiloé. Perhaps only a soft gleam crept in at first, like the dawn's earliest rays glinting over the Andes to the east.

Some days, a death cult (see Jer. 9:21) seemed to seep into every corner of every home from the humblest hovel to highest mansion, sucking up every drop of joy that didn't come from a jug. Year after year, I poured out the Water of Life. Especially to the young, the neediest and thirstiest.

*"I love to tell the story of unseen things above, of Jesus
and His glory, of Jesus and His love; I love to tell the*

*story, because I know 'tis true. It satisfies my longings as
nothing else could do..."*
–Katherine Hankey, hymn lyrics

I haven't an inkling of the impact of my life and work—
and may never have, this side of my home in heaven. Self-
validation spirals into a vain pursuit anyway, when only Jesus
really matters. But surely, for some, nightmares no longer haunt
the mists. I know that stories can change the world. And the
good news about Jesus has the power to change *everything*
from time to eternity. More than I can possibly comprehend.

Whether my words—spoken and unspoken—accom-
plished little or much, I'm convinced that a faith-infused story
that exalts Jesus can quite possibly achieve more for the kingdom of God than most theology books and doctrinal theses. It
only takes a spark… to ignite a leaping flame.

Today I *write* the stories. Sifting through the broken and
incoherent fragments around me, I'll rewrite the legends. May
God guide me to the nuggets of gold He wants me to find
and share.

For starters, I think of the character Angie De la Cruz's
escape to a better hope. While Melissa in *Destiny at Dolphin
Bay* describes "Señora Angélica" as a Chilote mermaid, in *Hope
Chest* we encounter the first faltering steps in her transformation from timid teenager to icon of courage—an island legend.

"If you want to change the world, pick up a pen," Martin
Luther said—and did. I made up my mind to discover the
treasures among the strange delusions of the world I lived in.
So I picked up a pen and, in this way, I offer my grain of sand,
my drop of ink, to change this world.

One simple tale at a time. Nothing wields more power.

Home Sweet Palafito

One of the most iconic scenes in the Chiloé Islands must surely be the alley of *palafitos*, picturesque houses built on weatherworn posts, that rises from a tidal flat to the right of the highway as you drive into the provincial capital of Castro. After lunch on the first afternoon of our anniversary trip back to Chiloé, we head for our own home sweet *palafito*.

A sweet *palafito*? I never thought of them that way when we lived in the islands. In fact, the outhouses perched at the end of their backyard "decks" and the reek of raw sewage as we drove by put me off. I never entirely realized, at that time, how unique and emblematic of Chiloé they are. After we left, this familiar vista of houses-on-stilts turned up everywhere in the country: Postcards, souvenir shops, even films.

Castro has several *palafito* neighborhoods besides the one at the entrance to the town. Some you'll find down on the main waterfront, past the Naval Administration. Along that same pot-holed street you'll see the Blue Unicorn, a rambling hillside hotel dressed in pinks and lilacs. It's a classic riot of Chilote color which I've always hankered to experience. But it's booked up this week, better luck next time.

Oh, and the unicorn? I can't tell you where that logo sprang from. Perhaps some imaginative islander modeled it on the Camahueto, a mythological marine bovine who transports witches to the ghost ship *Caleuche.*

Sweet Palafito

But as it happens, *palafito* tourism has become quite the rage in Chiloé these days. Of course, the plumbing's updated and the kerosene lanterns rewired now. Efficient but still charming slow-combustion Boscas have replaced the belching kitchen stoves. I've made a point of booking into as many different places as we could during the six days we have. So, naturally curious, we want to try out a home sweet *palafito.*

Back uphill and across a tidal flat from a big glass-roofed traditional hotel, ours is located in another fabled *palafito* neighborhood crowding the muddy estuary of Barrio Gamboa. The Palafito Azul (Blue Palafito) is a sort of rustic boutique apart-hotel (as they're called here) and wins the blue ribbon— our favorite of all the places we stay on this trip.

In the old days, *palafitos* wore the colors of seafood and salad: Pea green, mustard yellow, paprika, salmon, fiery *piure* orange. Usually faded and peeling. Today, their great variety of Chilote cedar shingles often maintains the dark gray of driftwood, with an annual paint job on the doors and window frames. You'll see turquoise and moss, lemon and fuchsia, perking up the trim. But if the shingles glow bright and resinous, you know they're brand new.

The Palafito Azul boasts sky-blue double front doors, set in a perfect silver wood jewel box. Each of its four suites consists of bedroom/bath and a kitchen/dining/living area.

Everything—floors, ceiling, walls, cupboards, and closet—is constructed of the same light natural wood, but instead of monotonous, the monochrome feels…soothing.

Peaceful Palafito

A trio of stained-glass windows sparkles in the bedroom. Long skeins of handspun yarn dangle from hooks in the hall. Dyed in lichen green, mushroom, and shades of woodsy browns, they blended seamlessly into the décor landscape.

The owner's daughter, a cheerful young woman fresh out of tourism school, lights the Bosca stove and leaves us toasting French bread for sandwiches. We take our tea snuggled under Chilote wool throws on a wide daybed next to the picture window. Its Gothic-arched frame, fitted with a balcony railing at the bottom, overlooks shallow milk-chocolate water and steps out into…nothing.

For a long time, we gaze at the sweeping vista of battered rowboats and fishing launches tipped on their sides in the mudflat. One by one, the town's lights pop out. You can look across the inlet to the warm golden twinkle of Castro. And it is so quiet.

> *"The devil has made it his business to monopolize on three elements: noise, hurry, crowds. He will not allow quietness."* –Elisabeth Elliot

We spend the evening reading, relaxing, resting. In the middle of writing *The Sea-Silk Banner*, I decide to word-paint the carved doors of Nicolás's house the same heavenly blue as the Palafito Azul's. If you've read *Destiny at Dolphin Bay*, you know the story homes in that book aren't sea-hugging *palafitos*.

But something of this perfect evening's calm weaves itself into the "dream house" scene of *Sea-Silk*.

Romantic Palafito

However, *Destiny at Dolphin Bay* does feature a street of *palafitos* in the fictional town of Mellehue. One of them, a rickety boarding home for students from the outer islands, collapses in the earthquake/tsunami mid-plot. Which leads Melissa, the main character, into involvement with the victims, a gaggle of traumatized little girls. No sweet *palafito*, that one.

> *"I could also see just by looking around me how we tend to over-romanticize history. Life in those other centuries had not been all knights-and-ladies stuff. There was nothing romantic about cottages where eight or ten people slept in one room with no privacy; where there were no bathrooms, not even outside privies—even if the cottage did happen to have picturesque thatch on the roof..."* –Catherine Marshall, *Christy*

But the character Leonel in *Legacy of the Linnebrink Light* inherits his legendary great-grandfather's grand *palafito* and uses it as a carpentry workshop—and refuge. A mystery whispers from the attic there...

For some (totally unplanned) reason, a lot of my recent reading has highlighted different types of historical and ethnic homes: Wigwams in colonial Maine, igloos in Alaska's not-so-distant past, the vast sheep ranches of the Argentine Patagonia worked by Chilote peasants for (often) European proprietors. The nomadic Yaghans who practically lived in their kayaks on the icy channels of Tierra del Fuego.

Shouldn't we all find sanctuary in our own home sweet *palafito*? In my series Swan Island Secrets, the character Coni flees to a cliff-hugging A-frame cottage. In Winds of Andalucía, Valeria seeks refuge in a Spanish *alcázar* (fortress-castle). And a century-plus ago, the Tierra del Fuego missionaries lived an abject existence in a land awesome in its barren beauty and merciless cold, their only sanctuary God Himself.

Palafito Sanctuary

One reviewer of *Destiny at Dolphin Bay* compares my book to *Christy* by Catherine Marshall. I'm fall-over-backwards thrilled, because Marshall's masterpiece was one of *the* important and influential books of my youth. *Christy* is a classic work of historical fiction based on her mother's life as a mission teacher in backwoods Appalachia one hundred years ago. And it made God real to me as a teen in rural Maine.

What does the novel *Christy* have in common with *Destiny at Dolphin Bay*? Of course some differences exist: Melissa, my main character, doesn't start out as a teacher or any kind of authority figure. She doesn't claim to offer any spiritual example or counsel. In fact, she's "escaped" from trouble back home to sanctuary with her sister in Chiloé.

But that said, I can see the many similarities: Both stories are "old-fashioned" historicals. I didn't write *Destiny at Dolphin Bay* as historical fiction, since it's set in my own lifetime and experience of the islands. Yet 1990 now places it squarely in today's past, illustrated by Chiloé's *palafito* culture. They're no longer home-sweet-shacks hovering over fetid mudflats but lucrative inns catering to those who'd like to try living in a boathouse.

Both stories take place in a rustic area, beautiful but isolated. At times frightening, at times as inviting and inspiring as a country retreat. Both stories feature a female lead character from a privileged home. Both are idealistic but naïve, comfortable in their shiny bubble world. (I liked Christy so much, however, that I believe I unconsciously gave a variation of her name to the main character of *Legacy of the Linnebrink Light*.)

In general, both stories portray the inhabitants of the "new world" as unsophisticated, uneducated, and superstitious. They range from kind and generous to mean and ugly. Most are simple in the best sense of the word: sincere, unpretentious.

Both stories relate a significant spiritual journey for the main character as well as for others. Both tell a tale about the God of love and hope and His touch on our lives in large and small ways. Melissa (of *Dolphin Bay*) certainly doesn't see herself as anyone special, yet like Christy, God has sent her to a place apart for a reason.

> *"For a few, the concept that life did not have to be all starkness and misery was slowly taking root. Tentatively, timidly—constantly encouraged...some of the women were at last reaching out for light and beauty and joy."*
> –Catherine Marshall, *Christy*

Palafito Symbols

While the symbolic home of Chiloé, the *palafito*, has mutated into a popular icon of the good life in the islands, my husband and I find the Palafito Azul a restful break for our hustled lives and harried souls this evening. Thank God for an old-fashioned home sweet *palafito*.

On the other hand, I'm learning that if the sanctuary isn't in my heart, it's hard to find. Home is where the Lord is, whether that's a castle in Spain, a cabin in the mountains of Tennessee, or a *palafito* by the Pacific. Like Christy and Melissa, I long for God's destiny, always so much better than any design of my own.

> *"Dear God," I said inside myself, "when I came here, maybe I was partly running off from home for fun and freedom and adventure. But I have a notion that You had something else in mind in letting me come. Anyway if You can use me here...well, here I am."*
> –Catherine Marshall, *Christy*

The World's Last Witch Trials

So *were* the Elders of the Righteous Province really witches? The whole idea seems like a creepy aberration from the backward past. What inferno ignited, then, in Ancud, Chiloé, in 1880? A witch hunt during the Industrial Age?

"It's just another old story," Nicolás Serrano insists to Melissa Travis in *Destiny at Dolphin Bay* as they debate the existence of a legendary ghost ship. He doesn't give much credence to the secret society of witches, either. But his grandmother Luisa would beg to differ, since *her* grandparents were caught up in the chilling drama of probably the world's last (and completely nonfictional) witch trials.

> *"Some things should not be forgotten."* –Elven Queen
> Galadriel, *The Fellowship of the Ring*

Witch hunts once cropped up regularly in the pages of history, from King Saul's hypocritical hounding of soothsayers and sorcerers in ancient Israel to the tragic Salem trials under the Puritans' covenant commonwealth (1692-93). But they had pretty much died out by the nineteenth century. Even the infamous Spanish Inquisition retracted its fangs by 1834.

So what set off Chile's down-played trials in 1880?

Politics, not religious persecution. Pursuing wartime renegades, not promoting righteousness.

Deserters and Devils

During the vicious South American conflict known as the War of the Pacific (1879-83), Chile fought for rich mining territory against a Peru-Bolivia alliance. In the meantime, Chile's traditional rival, Argentina, took advantage of the neighboring government's preoccupation in the northern desert to reassert old border claims in the south. Which led to the need for conscripting islanders, fierce homebodies who by far preferred hoes to rifles and fishing boats to artillery carts.

Naturally, that policy produced a *lot* of draft dodgers and army deserters.

Under pressure, the Governor of Chiloé ordered a round-up of these indigenous fugitives. As he tracked them down, he heard reports that some of those who harbored deserters also sheltered sorcerers in hidden caves. The members of this "Righteous Province" society of warlocks contended that *they* represented the legitimate native government.

The governor, an "enlightened" man of his times, hardly believed in witches. But he intended to root out seditious rebels and spies who claimed competition to the Republic of Chile. He would discover once and for all any truth behind the myths. So the witch trials originated in an attempt to get to the bottom of the Righteous Province *Mayores'* claim to exercise authority in the islands apart from the law of the land.

Agents of the central government rarely showed up outside Chiloé's two main towns, Castro and Ancud. So villagers, small farmers, and fishermen made easy prey for the warlock Elders and their personal ambitions and vendettas. By this time, the original revival—or perhaps perpetuation—of pagan customs had degenerated into a rural mafia that bred fear into the people in order to extort regular protection money.

Murder and Mayhem

The first trials grew out of concerns over an outbreak of suspicious poisonings, blamed on curses. Since many victims had been slain over the previous thirty years, one accusation and conviction led to another. As power struggles within the Righteous Province itself heated up and others took the opportunity for advantage or revenge, over 100 society members ended up arrested.

Although the trial transcripts of 1880-81 reveal supernatural allegations made by those on both sides of the proceedings, the court deemed at least a third of the cases to involve harmless native healers. Today many people claim that the so-called witch trials were twisted into nothing more than a crusade against the indigenous peoples and their cultural heritage. The merest whisper that an unpopular person might practice witchcraft offered sufficient cause to drag him off to the prisons of Ancud or Achao. (Echoes of Salem?)

But other researchers see the Elders of the Righteous Province as racketeers and assassins who had held the Islands of Chiloé hostage in a reign of terror for over a century. The provincial governor in Ancud put no stock in witchcraft and magic spells. But he was convinced that the men of the Righteous Province were thieves, outlaws, and murderers. They had spawned misery, hardship, and death for entire families and should be prosecuted to the full extent of the law.

For the record, the accused were *not* charged with witchcraft. That would have presented an embarrassment to the modern, albeit conservative, government of Chile. Instead, evidence of murders was cited. The self-styled warlocks were convicted of manslaughter and/or membership in an "unlawful society."

Dungeons and Dragons

Nobody got burned at the stake. Nobody got hanged on the gallows (as in Salem). A few, like the "witch king" Mateo Coñuecar, served brief prison sentences. However, the majority of the sentences imposed were soon overturned on appeal.

We can't take at face value any testimony at a witch trial. It's often spit out under duress. The Salem tragedy once again illustrates the point, as there some innocents "confessed" to save their lives.

On the other hand, most Chilotes at the time definitely viewed the members of the Righteous Province as not only valid witches, but as fearsome and powerful. While political ends sparked the trials more than any true piety, a strain of morbid fascination with the occult runs through the records.

Did witchcraft truly exist in Chiloé any more than in Salem? Possibly, but it's more likely that jealous slander and perjury kindled the conflagration of persecution in both places. An appetite for notoriety also provoked some performances. And fooling with the occult probably played as large a part as any true demonic possession or influence.

Beyond the contemporary politics and beneath the threads of economic exploitation, racism, and intolerance on myriad levels, the old dragon certainly lurked in Chiloé's dark corners and caverns back then. The governor may have thought he'd dispersed and defeated the Righteous Province for good. Conclusive evidence to the contrary is mysteriously lacking, too.

Nevertheless, I suspect most Chilotes still believe, in one way or another. In Angie De la Cruz's time, 1968. In Melissa and Nicolás's time, 1990. And to this day. Sometimes openly, enlisting in the ranks of revitalized societies embracing traditional religion or the current brand of back-to-the-earth.

Sometimes secretly, while scurrying through the woods on a misty evening...

The Hope Behind the Hunt

"Fairy tales are more than true: not because they tell us that dragons exist, but because they tell us that dragons can be beaten." –G.K. Chesterton

Can we triumph over the assaults of dragons and monsters?

Witch hunts have become little more than spine-tingling legends to most of us, a measure of imaginative fun as the tales get retold tongue-in-cheek around a campfire, in a class on folklore, or through folk songs such as *"La Bruja Voladora"* ("The Flying Witch"). Or in the local boats and ferries named in a nod to mythological figures. All of which reveal much about the dreams, desires, and dreads of a culture.

But when the authentic occult masquerades as folk beliefs, it's not entertainment. I understand the vague longings behind the legends. Wouldn't we all wish to live in a fairy-tale world of rags-to-riches, wishes-come-true, and love-conquers-all?

As much as we appreciate, even enjoy, the cultural heritage, we can't and don't embrace it without reservation. The devil shouldn't be revered but recognized for the roaring lion—murderer, liar, and thief—that he is without his disguises. His deceptions instigate much of life's unhappiness and unrighteousness. Whatever one's opinion of witch trials, that much was glaringly obvious even in 1880.

We live in a world at war. Ready or not, in Chiloé I stumbled into a spiritual battle for the souls of men and women. And recognize it or not, every child of God in every place is a warrior.

In these days of easy travel and quickie trips, the call to volunteer for a mission may start out cool, challenging, exciting even. Nobody mentions the long haul, the sacrifices, or—God forbid—the risks. I know nobody ever told me how scary and teary and tiring the fight would be.

But in Chiloé I began to understand that we God-followers exchange one thing for another: The life I planned for myself—the life I might have had—for the life God planned for me.

My problem is that somehow I believe it's not supposed to be this hard to keep slogging, keep praying, keep wielding my pen-for-a-sword. You can bet your combat boots, the endless march doesn't feel comfortable. After that initial moment of inspiration, I struggle every day. Maybe you do too.

We won't often receive many words of commendation either, let alone sweep up the medals. Like literally going to war, all we're given is *"a chance to die,"* as Elisabeth Elliot wrote of Amy Carmichael.

> *God always has a purpose. We always have a choice.*
> –Diana Delacruz

Our true hope of victory lies in the Sovereign Lord who came to *"render (the devil) powerless...and free those who through fear of death were subject to slavery all their lives"* (Heb. 2:14-15, NASB). May He give boldness to challenge the dragon's lies with truth, lay the old terrors to rest, and commit to win.

Let's proclaim different stories of...

> Good news for the poor
> Healing for the brokenhearted
> Freedom for the captives
> Grace for the oppressed
> Sight for the blind
> Release from darkness (Is. 61:1; Lk. 4:18-19),
> And the love of God which *"casts out fear"* (I Jn. 4:18, NASB).

The answer lies not in witch trials and spook hunts but in winsome testimonies about the True *Mayor*—our Elder Brother, the Ancient of Days. He is greater than all. And His goodness we can trust.

Building Projects

Everything's built up. That's what we notice most as we leave the *palafito* (cottage-on-stilts) where we've lodged in Castro and head for the village of Rilán. The Chiloé Islands feature many examples of architectural creativity, but today the road is lined with building projects.

For starters, we could have arrived at the two-year-old airport in Mocopulli, an overgrown intersection where the nine-kilometer stretch of road to Dalcahue branches off the island's main highway. We chose the drive-and-ferry over the flight, but who could ever have imagined the day when we didn't have to?

And for another thing, the new asphalt pavement runs smooth and impeccable beneath the tires of our rental car. So on Day 2, instead of the highway, we take the coastal drive between Castro and Dalcahue. Always our favorite from the perspective of picturesque charm, but when we lived in the area, we usually opted for the highway for the sake of saving time. You just couldn't race the clock on the washboard of the scenic route.

An old-fashioned grain mill works along this road. I wish we could take time to view the antique structure, but choices,

choices. A friend who toured Chiloé recently also told me about an amazing cascade hidden away in the hinterlands north off the same road. Another bucket list item. Because today we are on a research mission:

Target Rilán

The hamlet of Rilán lies on a peninsula off the beaten track of the shore road. *And I have never been there.* What would it have taken us to drive to it years ago? Ten minutes? Maybe more before the road was paved, but still. The name of the place always struck me as a sort of musical trill, so I've renamed it and put it into the building projects of my story world.

Rilán turns into Trilán and becomes Melissa Travis's first experience as a missionary teacher. It's the reimagined site of El Sacho Restaurant, watering hole for a handful of characters. And the setting of a musical celebration, a naval battle, a kidnapping, a couple of weddings, and at least two unsolved murders (all in the series First Mate's Log.) My story architecture's as imaginative as the Chilotes'.

"I call architecture frozen music."
–Johann Wolfgang von Goethe

As we rumble into the real-life village, it's raining as it can only do in Chiloé. A steady splash and smack on the windshield, streams flowing down the windows. Most of my photos will turn out gray and dull, but on the other hand, what could be more realistic?

To my surprise, Rilán isn't at all like I thought. For some reason, I've envisioned it something like the town of Chonchi, just south of Castro. Chonchi's enchanting architecture rises up from the fiord it hugs on three distinct levels. So my Trilán is more a blend of the two settings.

Road to Restoration

We follow the couple of gravel tracks out of the village. One leads up to a misty hillside lookout, crowned by a lone stand of trees. A flock of sheep—white, black, and spotted—prance in a glistening emerald meadow.

The other road meanders down to the shore, a muddy tidal flat piled with dingy rowboats and mounds of multi-colored fishing twine. A tumbledown shack, weathered to the shade of driftwood, slumps above the mudflat. Once, it might have hosted a *fogón*, a rustic shelter for barbecues and bonfires. Now it begs for repairs.

Back in the village, we circle the *plaza*. We find the school, the firefighters' unit, the cemetery, a handful of unusually attractive homes. And the local church, freshly painted in pristine white with a sky-blue roof and trim. A funeral service is in progress, so the doors under the beautiful arched portico are thrown wide open.

We step inside for a quick peek. Blinding white walls brighten the gray of the day (and perhaps the occasion). A simple altar occupies the front of the vast space. It could hold three times the population of the village under its domed blue ceiling, without crowding.

On the ferry the previous day, we'd learned of the current restoration program for Chiloé's world-heritage churches. Curiosity piqued, we dropped into the Castro cathedral for the first time while waiting for check-in at the Palafito Azul yesterday afternoon.

Castro's Cathedral

We'd never visited any of these churches when we lived here. For one thing, we aren't Catholics, but we also viewed them as dark, dank caverns. Huge barnlike structures that smelled of dust, damp, and smoky candles. Gothic fixer-uppers, frozen in a time centuries past.

This trip, we thought we'd like to see some of these building projects, at least from an architectural, historical, and cultural point of interest. With the restoration program, the iconic churches now look like Fabergé Easter eggs: Fancy boxes decorated in robin's egg, seafoam, Pacific blue, neon orange.

Unlike most of the others, which are entirely constructed of wood, the provincial capital's cathedral is clad in a crazy quilt of painted metal—corrugated zinc, embossed tin. This year, Castro's colors are lemon and grape, with pomegranate accents.

The aisles of the interior are arranged like a museum with models of the newly restored churches and chapels in glass cases. A remarkable transformation has taken place throughout the island.

Representative of timeless architecture and a unique cultural heritage, the church building projects are jewels in the countryside. How tragic that their traditional religious *fiestas* usually feature more drunkenness than devotion. More wanton revelry than worship.

Revisiting Dalcahue

We leave Rilán in a meditative mood, wondering how much has changed in Chiloé. Wouldn't it be wonderful to find

renewed hearts along with restored shells? I pray the renovated exteriors mean an inner reality of redemption rather
than the same old with a skin-deep paint job.

Or are they like the concrete pylons spiking up from the
channel seas, symbolic of a bridge project begun in hope but
abandoned stillborn?

Do the building projects resemble the quintessential
Chilote gorse bushes choking the ditches and fields, just
now at the height of their buttercup-yellow blooms? Oh, so
impressive. But an illusion? Deceptive thorns beneath the
flower show?

More novel projects await us all along the road to
Dalcahue. Dalcahue is our hometown in Chiloé. Combined
with elements from the town of Achao (on the neighboring
island of Quinchao), it forms the backdrop and prototype for
Mellehue, the main town in *Destiny at Dolphin Bay* and my
story universe in the first two series.

Like Mellehue, Dalcahue's the principal port to and from
the outer islands of the archipelago. For this reason, we settled
here and took up the reins—or sails—of ministry responsibil-
ities in the mid 1980's.

But it's become another place now. Blossomed, burgeoned,
burst? Not yet sure if it feels good or bad, we wind through the
streets, wide-eyed and wowed.

No more tin-sided shacks and two- or three-room shan-
ties like the Pérez family whacks up in *Dolphin Bay* after the
earthquake. Just down from the soccer field and the municipal
gymnasium, tsunami evacuation signs poke up at every corner.
(Afterthoughts from the 2010 quake.) A warren of streets jam
the hills. Dalcahue Heights, it's called. High-falutin' name for

a *población* (in Chile, a neighborhood packed with low-cost, sardine-can homes). Talk about a population tidal wave.

Then and Now

Dalcahue's church on the town *plaza* is encased stairs-to-steeple in wooden staging. Their renovation is in still process, apparently. Hard to imagine it anything but weathered black, as in Melissa's time, but I hope they decide on an appealing shade of blue. Not Dijon mustard, knock on wood.

> *"A man should hear a little music, read a little poetry,*
> *and see a fine picture every day of his life, in order that*
> *worldly cares may not obliterate the sense of the beautiful*
> *which God has implanted in the human soul."*
> –Johann Wolfgang von Goethe

We turn east out of town and cover the road to San Juan, where we used to take our girls for a Friday evening run on the gray pebbled beach. Now the road connects with another and goes all the way to Tenaún. I blended those two places to create Flamingo Beach in my story world.

It's every bit as built up now as in my books. You'll see Ricardo Treviño's new fishery, the lighthouse where (spoiler!) the characters Melissa and Nicolás fall in love, and scores of houses old—and new, like Tito's mother's cottage.

Well past lunch time, we hurry back to check out the food offerings on the Costanera, or waterfront street. We've been told the old Sunday open-air market has boomed into a thriving tourist complex, but we didn't hear the half.

This entire street, like the town of Curaco de Vélez on Quinchao, still displays the classic architectural whimsy of the islanders. At the far end, near the ferry ramp, the ancient, shingled houses are renowned and photographed for their striking oddities and quirky angles. In Curaco, they hint of haunted houses. Friends of ours lived in one where crocheted curtains hung like spider webs in the windows.

Favorite Spots

Closer to the dock of artisanal fishing launches, the mildewed facades used to sag down to open almost directly onto the sidewalk. You wouldn't have found any *palafitos* back then, except a restaurant that popped up near the end of our time there, but plenty of seedy *cantinas*.

As Dalcahue's rarest and prettiest structure, I always voted for the office of the port captain (or harbormaster). The two-story place, if you can imagine it, resembled a ship with a white corrugated-metal "hull," balconied "decks," and gingerbread trim in black or navy.

I loved the port captain's residence so much that it makes at least a cameo appearance in almost every book I've written. Sometimes it even comes close to center stage—when the character Nicolás becomes *capitán de puerto*, for instance.

Today we find the trim a snappy cherry red. A HOSTEL sign hangs out front. Maybe it no longer belongs to the harbormaster. At any rate, it can have no connection with official Navy business anymore. Sigh…

But the tourist trade flourishes with *sandwicherías* and craft shops galore. We can take our pick of these building projects.

So we duck out of the drizzle into a *palafito* community kitchen with round windows like portholes and unfinished wooden shiplap walls. At a counter along one side, we devour *curanto en olla*, or *pulmay*, clambake-in-a-pot. The Chilote version includes smoked pork, sausages, *milcao* (crackling-filled potato patties), and dumpling-like bread, as well as clams and mussels of all sizes. But that's a fish tale for another day.

Bright Future

The one spot we don't linger near today is our own former yard up Mocopulli Avenue. The Bible Center church, now boasting a smart iron street-front fence, looks otherwise unchanged. But a housefire destroyed our old home a few years ago. We'll tour the replacement tomorrow.

As we head back toward Castro, I think: What about my building projects? The architecture of my life and dreams? Under the allure of the latest blueprints and modern techniques, am I bumping into the same hard angles? A new look so often means just the old concepts recycled.

Not all tradition's trash, by a long shot. But some of it needs a wrecking ball instead of a reno. The fluff and stuff of wood, hay, and stubble takes up a lot of space that I could better fill with the treasures of gold, silver, and precious stones. There, a little stretches a long way, I believe.

More than two centuries ago, well-meaning friends of the Father of Modern Missions begged him to stick with the tried-and-true spiritual projects in his own backyard. His famous reply:

> *"I'm not afraid of failure. I'm afraid of succeeding at things that don't matter."* –William Carey

In Dalcahue, our home burned, but the church remains. Yet…did we construct on sand or solid Rock? God help us to see past the paint to the people. To look beyond the impressive buildings to the blessing of transformed lives.

After we drive through Castro and head south, we'll pass the new Enjoy Hotel. We've chosen not to stay at this five-star country cousin of the Ritz. Instead, we plan to spend the night at a cabin in Trilán. Oops, I mean, Chonchi. Or maybe it's Chonchi Heights.

A Legend of the Flood

Both *Destiny at Dolphin Bay* as well as one of my current projects, *Hope Chest*, feature a background of Chilote mythology. It shouldn't surprise us that the myths of a territory such as the Chiloé Islands, surrounded by ocean, should commence with an epic battle between land and sea, represented by two great serpents.

Though this traditional story doesn't appear in my books, it underlies much of the worldview of Chiloé. In different clothes, the "legend" of a universal flood exists in almost every culture of the world, from the Chinese to the Babylonians to the Incas. The Chilotes, pummeled by near daily rain, present no exception. In their legend of the flood, a pair of snakes symbolizes our eternal Enemy.

The Chiloé version turns the worldwide flood into a surprisingly plausible theory of the geological origins of the archipelago, an explanation of their amphibious (land and sea) island culture, and a fierce struggle between good and evil, which, after all, is what the best stories are made of.

Land and Sea

In the beginning…the myth assumes creation. At present, the island province of Chiloé consists of one large island (about one-third more square mileage than Prince Edward Island, Canada) and a scattered swarm of medium-sized and tiny islands. But thousands of years ago, the archipelago formed part of a single land mass connected to the South American continent.

According to Chilote mythology, the island group springs from the battle between two mighty serpents, Tentén-vilu and Coicoi-vilu. Tentén-vilu (from *ten* – "earth" and *vilu* – "snake," in the indigenous tongue of the Huilliches) is the spirit or goddess of the earth. Coicoi-vilu (*co* – "water") is, of course, the spirit of the water, specifically the seas.

The earth goddess, Tentén (or Treng-treng, in some accounts), represents the positive forces of abundance, fertility, and all that grows and flourishes on land, especially human beings. The water/sea goddess, Coicoi (or Cai-cai), on the other hand, represents the negative forces of the universe and every evil thing that lurks in the ocean depths. Together, these mythical reptiles personify the conflict between earth and sea, beneficent and maleficent powers.

The good spirit watches over and protects her dominions from the ever-threatening invasions of the sea. The enemy of human and terrestrial life ever desires *"to steal and kill and destroy"* (Jn. 10:10, NASB).

War of the Worlds

One fateful day, without warning, Coicoi appears in the form of a monstruous snake and declares a cosmic war on the land. Obeying her command, the fountains of the deep rise rapidly, inundating the lowlands and valleys, drowning most of the inhabitants. When the flood waters have nearly buried the hills and mountaintops of the entire region, Tentén arrives on the scene.

The counterattack comes not a moment too soon. As the protectress-serpent launches an assault against her enemy, she elevates the land and aids men, women, and beasts in reaching higher ground. To some men, Tentén gifts the ability to fly or transforms them into birds or sealions. Animals she turns into stones.

The struggle between these two forces persists, long nip-and-tuck, terrible and tenacious. Neither rival demonstrates clear supremacy. Tentén manages to prevail, but only in the sense of halting the enemy's advance. The lost "paradise" is never completely, categorically, regained.

Coicoi fails in her bid to overpower the heights. The rain stops, the waters subside. Yet few people are saved from the great catastrophe, and the battlefields never return to their original limits. The once-fruitful dales and vales remain sub-merged, transformed into gulfs and channels. The hills and mountain peaks become islands, large and small, their stony soil and rocky shores woven together by an intricate network of canals.

From this legend of the flood, the incomparable Archipelago of Chiloé emerges.

Geologically speaking, the current characteristics of southern Chile provide some evidence of the cataclysmic event that this myth relates. You only have to glance at a map to appreciate how Chile's central valley peters out at the extreme end of the Province of Llanquihue, on the mainland just north of Chiloé. Perhaps better said, the valley maintains its same trajectory *under the sea* (*Llanquihue* means "sunken place"). The coastal mountain range shatters into a multitude of islands.

Just and Justifier

In the cosmogeny of indigenous Chiloé, the formation of the island group via a drawn-out war between land and sea creates the area's basic lifestyle. And consequently, its peculiar mythology, traditional magic, and deep-rooted customs. The legend of the flood symbolizes their view of the world as an ongoing battle between the principles of good and evil.

But is that reality? Of course, we long for the triumph of justice and truth, what we call "good." We wish for the defeat of the powers of evil, the main cause of pain and grief in this unhappy world.

Yet what fascinates me to the point of goosebumps is that *both* the forces of this story represent God. You can immediately see the connection with Tentén, the giver and caretaker of life, the savior. But Coicoi also plays a part. Not that God does evil—He is good and intends good in all situations.

But in the book of Genesis, *God* sends the flood. The waters rise at His command. He is both the fearsome punisher and the ultimate protector. There is no clashing dichotomy here. As always, God hates the sin and loves the sinner. He demands righteousness—and then provides it.

> *"Mercy and truth have met together; Righteousness and peace have kissed"* –Ps. 85:10, NKJV

Romans 3:25-26 (NKJV) tells us: *"God had passed over the sins...to demonstrate...His righteousness, that He might be just and the justifier of the one who has faith in Jesus." "...Justified by faith, we have peace with God..."* (Rom. 5:1, NKJV). This peace treaty with God, this *shalom*, means much more than the absence of conflict. It carries the connotation of healing, wholeness, prosperity, and well-being.

Even for our friends in rural Chiloé, the good life must start with being good with God. Merely opposing some obvious brand of wickedness and supporting positive values won't elevate our souls or bring about victory over the Evil One.

Righteousness and Peace

On the other hand, *neither* of these mythological spirit forces is like our God. He doesn't settle for a draw, pull off halfway rescues, or compromise with evil. He is always the victor, never the vanquished.

The Great Snakes' legend of the flood misses the mark entirely. Fear of the diabolical enemy of humanity abounds and still inundates the Archipelago of Chiloé. An ambivalent sense of blind fate haunts these islands, a never-dissipating terror of the dark and unknown forces of nature.

At the end of the struggle of the serpents, Coicoi slinks away into the depths, leaving as her envoy an aquatic creature born during the flood. El Millalobo, as he/it is known, becomes the absolute *"prince of the power"* of the sea. Supposedly.

For those modern Chilotes who don't necessarily believe in ancient gods they must please and appease, the need to outwit or outmaneuver others still guides daily life to some extent. Traditional tricks to hide flaws, save face, or just keep one's neck above the religious waters lurk behind many social conventions and community celebrations.

It's so tempting to give up and call a truce. Or to give in to half a victory, to the wishful thinking that fulfilling the minimum requirements constitutes a winning strategy. We all deceive ourselves whenever we believe that maintaining the status quo, doing our "duty," will gain us true success.

> *"When the powers of darkness are arrayed against you and aim to destroy your joy forever, nothing is more precious than to have the Word of God ready for the battle. The fight for joy is NOT for the unarmed."*
> –John Piper

Our glorious salvation...

...never means simple survival in a fallen, flooded world. All of us, including the islanders, *"who through fear of death were subject to slavery all their lives"* (Heb. 2:15, NASB), can move from brokenness to blessedness. We sink, but we can learn to swim because *"the weapons of our warfare are not of the flesh, but divinely powerful"* (2 Cor. 10:4, NASB) and because *"the Son of God appeared for this purpose, to destroy the works of the devil"* (I Jn. 3:8, NASB). Victory!

Whether on land or sea, *"the Lord will rescue me from every evil deed, and will bring me safely to His heavenly kingdom"* (2 Tim. 4:18, NASB). We are redeemed, restored, and renewed. In the true legend of the flood, the Sun of righteousness wins.

> *"Thanks be to God who gives us the victory through our Lord Jesus Christ"* –I Cor. 15:57, NASB

Time in a Bottle

In the Chiloé Islands, the more things change, the more they stay the same. *"Everything changes…"* echoes a folksong I referenced in *Destiny at Dolphin Bay*. And I realize it's true: You just can't keep time in a bottle.

My husband and I have spent the day in Rilán, a coastal village I fictionalized as Trilán in *Legacy of the Linnebrink Light* and the First Mate's Log series. Though the place looks different than I expected, I'd never been there before so can't say what, if anything, has changed in twenty years. But we also visited the market town of Dalcahue, where we lived and called home through the '80's and early '90's, and… everything *has* changed. Time didn't stay in a bottle, for sure.

So we pause for supper in the island capital of Castro at a restaurant we've never seen before, let alone checked out. To our surprise, the two-story Café and Grill of the Firemen's Brigade takes the prize as the best new food stop of the trip. The menu offers fresh variations on familiar sandwiches. We sample a version of *chacareros*—Chile's green-bean-and-shaved-beef classic—while studying the décor of firefighting equipment on the fire-engine-red walls.

Time Overnight

Then we drive the twenty minutes south of Castro to the town of Chonchi, where we'll spend the night at the Treng-Treng Cabins (named for Tenten-vilu, the earth serpent who "saved" Chiloé from the flood). It's dark by the time we arrive, so we don't appreciate the quaint tangerine wood cottages overlooking the Fiord of Castro until sunrise the next morning.

But we can snuggle in next to the Bosca stove for an evening of reading. The rustic resort's manager comes to light the fire for us and chats for a few minutes. Turns out he's a Christian from Santiago, and he not only knows of the church we plan to visit tomorrow, he and his family also attend there every other weekend when he's not on duty. With the constant influx of newcomers to Chiloé now, the population doesn't stay stuck in a bottle either.

Day 3. We have little time for savoring Sunday leisure and coffee the next morning. The services in Dalcahue start early and we have nearly an hour's drive to get north and east of Castro. But we pull into the grassy church yard just in time.

And of course, it's different. What else did we expect? The street front fence displays a row of elegant iron stakes instead of painted pickets these days. Inside, a partition has disappeared, leaving a single spacious room, and the walls now wear my favorite shade of sky blue.

Time Warp

But after I take a second look, I notice the wooden floors still gleam with an impeccable Chilote wax job. The mullioned windows hold the same exquisite, pebbled glass. And those golden pews? My husband made them with his own hands and varnished them while he hobbled on crutches following a chainsaw accident in 1984.

The exterior is the same pale yellow and black. The overgrown lawn is still greener than emeralds. And the *mañío* trees we planted have only grown taller than the church building. Not that much has changed.

And we're okay with what has. It's wonderful to see our former Chilean co-workers, Miguel and Marisa, and Raimundo and Paulina.* I recognize Marisa's daughters. I've known them since they were born, and now they're young women. I *don't* realize at first that's Raimundo and Paulina's youngest son leading the service. Kids sure don't stay in a bottle, as much as we'd sometimes like to stop time.

Then there's Señora Laura and Señora Elizabeth,* both their husbands drunken bullies back then…and probably still. But their families are grown up. My oldest daughter used to wander the school halls with Laura's son during religion class (the only other *canuto*, or evangelical). Now the once-chubby boy stands tall and handsome and brings his own son to Sunday school.

Elizabeth's son, who pinched whatever he could get away with from our home as a teenager, is now an elder of the church and the happiest man in town. Oh, *thank God* neither time nor tragedies remain in a bottle for thirty years! The Dalcahue church has blossomed with a vibrant missionary vision for reaching the outer islands.

Time Table

Raimundo and Paulina invite us home for lunch. Of course they do. Even though they're not expecting us and have nothing prepared. We've known them long enough to consider them like our own kids. In fact, Rai came to us as a single Bible college intern our last year in Chiloé, preparing to replace us when the time was right.

He's the pastor now. Goosepimply amazing, this guy could've been—or done—or studied anything he desired. He's a gifted leader, whip smart, had star potential. Yet he's poured it all out in the "godforsaken" islands of Chiloé.

She used to glitter in Santiago, the life of every party. Sparked riots and rebellions. Now she's one of the funniest, sweetest, and godliest women I know. Nope, God doesn't keep any of us in a bottle.

We are delighted to tour their new house, a white island-style Cape Cod constructed on the charred foundation of the old and still a work in progress. Cantaloupe-colored walls surround the ubiquitous wood-burning stove. Which feels perfect as Paulina pulls out all the stops for a meal of baked chicken and ice cream with wafer cookies.

We sit around the table talking and drinking *mate* from a gourd and straw all afternoon. And enjoying the same window view of the town that shows up in *Destiny at Dolphin Bay* and in a watercolor hanging in my home to this day.

Time in a bottle, for a few hours at least.

Time Heals

Just before dark, we say our good-byes and make a final tour of Dalcahue. Sigh… Even the jewel-box mansion that I made the character Delicia's house in my books has changed. As surely as it does in the story when Angélica moves in and transforms it into a homey castle. Its varnished timbers used to wear a golden glow, but today the once-monochromatic wood flaunts a cloak of colonial red trimmed with sage green. Fleur-de-lis finials crown the iron fence.

As we pass the ferry slip for the neighboring island of Quinchao, I ask myself, *Why did we decide* not *to go over there on this trip?* Years ago, we crossed to the towns of Curaco de Velez and Achao at least once a week. Almost a second home to us.

The excuse of familiarity rings hollow. Of course, our time is short, and we want to focus on places we know less well. On the other hand, I have a feeling I'm evading the memory of stormy events there. (And not just the 1984 attempt on Pinochet.)

It's the parsonage swindle and the stolen church offerings. The cool reception from some high school students. A lovely Christian teen's affair with a married man. Her brother's crumbled university dreams. The bickering among believers. So many disappointments…

Yet now that it's too late, I wish we'd made the effort. Because, though Achao dragged more than its share of missionaries down a sinkhole… though a missionary baby as well as a bleeding host of missionary ideals lie buried and forgotten there… though untold tears spilled into that bitter bottle, it's still the town of *Calle Delicias*. The Street of Delicious Things. Delectable delights.

Where every sour worm can be made sweet, every sorrow turned into joy. I *need* to remember the picnics, the tea parties, the summer clambakes, and the winter hog slaughters. The music, the scenery, the laughter to the bottom of my belly. And the time I stood at the tip of Quinchao Island, stunned and certain I'd discovered the most beautiful spot on earth.

> *"Sometimes you will never know the value of a moment until it becomes a memory."* –Theodore Seuss Giesel

A place where every impoverished heart can be made rich and full. Where around every bend you find another story, another character, another snippet for the storehouse of the soul.

I regret I've missed this chance to revisit Achao. To dump out the old bottles and refill them with new experiences. Because time heals all hurts, they say. I wonder, but...

Time Will Tell

And if time doesn't heal, then God surely will.

Sometimes He teaches us through time, too. Upon arrival back in Castro, we check into our next hotel room. And wow, time's corked up in a bottle here. Back in the '80's, this Hotel* meant big bucks, *the* classy place to stay in town. I always admired the huge windows in the steep-sloped black roof. But we should have suspected something had changed—or *not* changed with the times—when it was so affordable.

A wannabe-elite ambience still lingers in the lobby and lounge, like the vintage charm of a country estate gone to seed.

But our room hasn't seen an update in decades and definitely lacks appeal. Lesson learned today: Don't chase the good memories, don't run from the bad. Make new ones.

> *"By trying to grab fulfillment everywhere, we find it nowhere."* –Elisabeth Elliot

Do you ever wish the world would stop and the wonderful things in our lives would remain always the same? The children would stay small and cute, the romance would continue to burn bright, the good times roll on forever? But you can't keep time in a bottle. You can't live like a genie in a bottle, either.

And even if you *could* save your days in a bottle, would you? Maybe it's enough to know that God catches our tears in *His* bottle and sprinkles them out in the sacrifice of praise. We can't bottle our happy moments or keep our cracked vessels from leaking. But He can fill us again and again.

Time Change

And He does tonight, as we return to the Firemen's Grill. We try another fancy sandwich and drink coffee with milk-foam hearts. I'm so inspired here that eventually this snack shop will wind its way into the climax of *The Sea-Silk Banner*, the finale of Melissa Travis's saga begun in *Destiny at Dolphin Bay*.

The message in our bottle reads: *Everything changes. Hold time loosely, eternity's coming.* I recall my surprise when I learned "Everything Changes" was an Argentine song that my Chilote teens sang. Lots of things blow across the *pampas* and over the Andes. Songs don't stay in a bottle any more than time and change.

But God transforms broken bottles to sea glass.

*Names in this chapter have been changed or omitted.

The Little Mermaid

In my daughter's recent university graduation photos, she poses with friends and classmates from around the world, a fascinating and varied ensemble of colors and cultures, ethnicities and languages. As a holder of triple citizenship herself, she barely notices but instead integrates the differences into her multiverse. Amazingly, she's never seemed to suffer from an identity crisis, even since dressing up as a mermaid in kindergarten.

Who am I, after a lifetime in Chile? As a combination of every place I've ever lived, perhaps a better question is: Who have I become? And who are my third-culture kids? TCKs grow up a blend of the home country, the host country, and another culture entirely their own. Yet the dual or multiple loyalties don't usually result in "split personalities," either in the sociopolitical arena or in the spiritual realm.

My "mermaid" daughter knows who she is. If an identity crisis exists, it's more often because she resists pigeonholing. Is she Chilean or American or Canadian? She is all and none of the above.

"By the grace of God, I am what I am," declared Paul, the Jewish apostle to the Gentiles (I Cor. 15:10, NASB). Our Lord Jesus Christ, Son of God and Son of man, would agree.

> *"There was no identity crisis in the life of Jesus Christ. He knew who He was... where He had come from, and why He was here. And He knew where He was going. And when you are that liberated, then you can serve."*
> –Howard G. Hendricks

In a previous chapter, I shared the story of the conflict between the two great serpents. According to Chilean mythographer and physician, Dr. Bernardo Quintana Mansilla, this is the foundational legend in Chilote mythology. It concludes with the birth of El Millalobo, ruler of the oceans. The tale continues with his three royal merchildren.

Daughter of Earth and Sea

Once upon a time, the golden-furred Millalobo took a wife. (His name comes from *milla* – "gold" in Huilliche, and *lobo* – Spanish for "wolf"; in this case, a *lobo marino* is a sea lion.) Huenchula, the daughter of a Chilote woodsman and a well-known witch (or witch doctor, *machi*), lived near the banks of the river flowing from Lake Cucao to the Pacific Ocean, on the remote western shore of the Big Island of Chiloé.

The industrious girl undertook all the household chores, since her mother dedicated most of her time to the practice of her "profession," which included gathering herbal remedies and tending to her "clients." But one day, Huenchula vanished on her daily walk to the nearby lake for water. Bewitched by

El Millalobo, she eloped to sea with him, leaving no trace except an empty bucket, much to the anguish of her parents.

A year later, Huenchula reappeared at her parents' home, bearing gifts from her husband—a powerful king, she explained—as well as a newborn daughter cradled in a limpet shell. She would not permit her elders to look upon their grandchild (don't ask me why). However, when she stepped outside for a moment, they couldn't resist and sneaked a peek!

Instantly, the baby girl was transformed into a puddle of crystalline water. Upon her return, the mother snatched up the limpet, ran away again, and gently emptied the watery remains of her child into the ocean depths. Overcome with grief, Huenchula recounted the tragedy to her husband.

No sooner had she finished the tale when a dainty boat resembling a limpet shell floated toward her. Out stepped her recently liquified daughter, transformed into a lovely young woman of incomparable charm and sweetness. Her parents named her Pincoya (or Piñuda, from *pinda* – "hummingbird," plus *colún* – "reddish color").

Children of Dual Heritage

El Millalobo, as viceroy of the sea serpent Coicoi-vilu, generously offers his bounty of fish and shellfish to the people of the Chiloé Islands. He sows on their coasts and in their seas through his favorite daughter, the golden-haired Pincoya. On her good graces depends the abundance—or shortage—of seafood in the channel waters.

In Chilote mythology, La Pincoya is a goddess of extraordinary beauty who personifies the fertility of the seas and seashores. Periodically, she emerges from the depths, semi-dressed in a skirt of ropy algae, to dance on the gravel beaches or upon the waves. Unlike the fabled mermaids, both her arms and legs resemble those of an ordinary human being. And she is said to be so attractive that even the fishes' mouths gape.

When La Pincoya performs her dance facing the high seas, this means that fish and shellfish will abound in the area. On the other hand, if she dances with her face turned toward shore, this indicates that fish will become scarce.

If the scarcity persists over a long period, La Pincoya has become displeased because of careless or uncontrolled over-fishing. She can be persuaded to return her favor through the intervention of a *machi* in a magic ceremony. Only the *machi* has the power to convince her to grant abundance again.

When the islanders shipwreck, La Pincoya hastens to their rescue, accompanied by her siblings…

El Pincoy and La Sirena

A bit of an identity crisis exists in the story here, as all three share a somewhat similar appearance and perform different facets of the same task.

Because of his fascination with music, El Pincoy's alternate name is Pincullhue (meaning "flute"). The stories usually describe him as a creature with the body of a huge silvery seal and the face of a handsome man with a mane of golden hair.

La Sirena (the Spanish word for mermaid) looks and dresses practically identical to her sister. She specializes in caring for her father's sea creatures as a sort of marine shepherdess. Fortunate fishermen may catch an occasional glimpse of her among the rocks, combing her long red-gold locks. And once, so the tale goes, she got tangled in a net and sobbed in distress until the fisherman took pity and released her.

Mixed Myths

I've garnered much of my education in Chilote mythology from Dr. Quintana's book, *Chiloé Mitológico*. The late author/investigator (1916-2012) was born and raised in the town of Achao, on the island of Quinchao. Later, his pioneering use of x-ray technology earned him the reputation of a warlock in the Chiloé of the 1940's! I wonder if, as a man of science, he experienced an identity crisis when visiting home?

In the preface of his book, Dr. Quintana expresses that in researching the legends of Chiloé, he never purposed *"to revive superstitions nor to return to belief in witches, mysterious powers, or magic forces, but ... to offer it to all those restless minds who may use it as a source of inspiration in their new creations."* He himself hand-carved a museum-quality collection of mythological scenes, like the craftsman character Leonel in *Legacy of the Linnebrink Light*.

Many people believe that Chilote myths exist in various forms in other places and have been imported through the conquistadores, pirates, or travelers. While this suggestion has merit, in most cases the stories intermingled with indigenous legends to the point of blurring the boundary lines.

The myth of La Pincoya corresponds more or less to the Nereids, or sea nymphs of European waters. And perhaps to other fertility goddesses of Egyptian, Greek, and Roman mythologies.

Another strange identity crisis pops up between La Pincoya and El Pincoy, as the tale sometimes connects them as siblings and at other times as spouses. In this case, it's possible the legend of El Millalobo and La Huenchula is duplicated in their children. Alternatively, Pincoy/Pincoya may represent male and female manifestations of the same spirit of fertility.

The idea of legend duplication also evidences when we compare La Pincoya and La Sirena. Their main difference is that, in place of legs and feet, the younger mermaid sister possesses a fish's tail and glittering silver scales on her lower body.

As a medical professional, Dr. Quintana surmises that the infrequent births of infants with *sirenomelia* (AKA mermaid syndrome) gave rise to the myth of mermaids (and mermen). Generally, these children survive only a few hours or days, but this rare congenital anomaly genuinely occurs (1/100,000 births). I wonder if it's more common in secluded areas such as the islands where consanguineous hook-ups frequently occur?

Mermaid Mosaic

Often considered wicked temptresses, the sirens of many mythologies utilize their beautiful singing voices to lure unsuspecting sailors to their deaths on rocks and reefs. In contrast, Hans Christian Andersen's broken-hearted *Little Mermaid* leaps to her death after failing to win the prince's love (and a human soul).

While Disney exchanged the older versions for lighter, happier fare, I think they still got it wrong. Though their mermaid's father demands she abandon her love for a human, instead she sacrifices her mermaid privileges to gain a human life with him. She has to decide for land or sea, air or water.

Instead of either/or, why we can't we enjoy both/and?

As with my Third-Culture Kids, an identity crisis doesn't have to erupt when you choose to be simply who you are. Or rather, who God has designed you to be. Though TCKs sometimes deal with the confused loyalties of "belonging everywhere and nowhere," they recognize their birthrights of global connection, expanded worldview, and linguistic adeptness.

Who are any of us but the awesome combination of our genes, our habits, and our choices?

The masterpiece of personal identity as a child of the Now-but-Not-yet Kingdom begins with delighting in and using to the glory of God each piece of the puzzle that makes up the person you and I become. In His plan, we aren't born when and where we are without a reason. We don't go through unique experiences just because. Rather than give up these life components or throw them away, God means to integrate them all into an *"immense orchestra of earth, sky, and sea"* (*Destiny at Dolphin Bay*).

A concert, not a crisis.

Integrated Identity

Who is the character Melissa Travis? In *Destiny at Dolphin Bay*, she learns that God has molded her into far more than just herself or her family or school, or even the sum of her background parts.

Where does her friend Nicolás truly feel at home? In the cosmopolitan capital, like his father? Or on the rustic island, like his mother? His search for identity leads him to *both* worlds, leaping effortlessly like his pod of pet dolphins between water and air.

And beyond, as all children of God, citizens of heaven on earth. *"When you are that liberated, you can serve,"* Professor Hendricks reminds us.

Locals call Nicolás's mom, Angélica, *La Sirenita*—the little mermaid girl. These days I'm writing the *why*, the memory behind the myth, in *Hope Chest*. Who is Angie De la Cruz and how does she morph into the White Lady of Chauquelín? Before her story ends, she must exercise every gift, employ every resource she possesses, to raise a generation that will change her island's future forever.

"Christians have a dual citizenship—on earth and in heaven—and our citizenship in heaven ought to make us better people here on earth." –Warren Wiersbe

So I'm taking Dr. Quintana at his word and using the mythology of Chiloé as a source of inspiration. For stories rather than visual art, in my case.

Stories of tragedies turned into tales of triumph. Disasters to diamonds. Teardrops to oceans of love-that-trusts and faith-that-works.

Stories of transformation from jagged glass to beautiful jewels…via many a stormy passage that culminates in a joyful dance upon the waves.

Light Years from My Comfort Zone

Back in the decade we lived in the Chiloé Islands, a hippie sort of bookshop lay tucked between our favorite restaurant, El Sacho, and the Castro hotel where we've just spent the night. The place was called *Light Years*, and this morning as I wake up, I still feel light years out of my comfort zone here.

Light Years's windows were crammed not only with books on subjects ranging from metaphysics to local lore, but also boasted crystals, pyramids, incense, and anything else left over from the Chilean Age of Aquarius. Despite the (perhaps superficial?) changes we've observed here during our visit, I wonder, as I often used to, if real transformation still crawls light years in the distance.

It's Day 4 of our Return to Chiloé anniversary trip, and today, a Monday this year, is the actual date. We aren't particularly thrilled with this rundown ex-VIP hotel we've spent the night at. But we rise to the occasion, determined to make everything special even if some of it's out of our comfort zone.

Morning Mist

For some reason I can't quite identify, the dining room feels homey this morning as we have our breakfast. Maybe it's the soothing crackle and the woodsy smoke from the open fireplace with its hammered iron hood. Or the aroma of fresh rolls and coffee, the pots of yogurt and dishes of blackberry jam. It could even be the call from family in Santiago that we enjoy as we linger over a second *café con leche*.

Possibly we hang out longer at the table because one of the most spectacular scenes of the trip spreads out before our dewy window. Before today, we've only ever visited this restaurant after dark, and how much we missed! Gigantic Araucanian pines (AKA monkey puzzles) frame the ice-blue finger of the Fiord of Castro in feathery-ink relief. White cotton puffs dot the sky. A rainbow of roofs tumbles toward the inlet waters. So we make new memories.

A cruise ship has docked in the port below, and a gaggle of seniors is herded into the hotel for brunch just now. We're glad to slip away as the dining room clogs up. Their tourist guidebook needs updating, we think, or somebody has clout since Castro offers far more interesting places to visit. They'll appreciate the view here, at least, and it gives us a smile to realize we're not the only ones out of our comfort zone today.

Rainy Days and Mondays

Almost as soon as we drive out of the hotel parking lot, the morning fog condenses into drizzle and envelops us. We wander around the town, revisiting old haunts and recounting tales of long-ago problems and pleasures. The weather only gets disconcertingly worse. Soon it's raining cats and dogs, exclusive Chiloé style.

After living in Santiago for so many years, we've all but lost our skills for dealing day after day with rain, rain, rain. Maybe we've forgotten we won't melt, because we're content to stay cozy in the comfort zone of our rental car, even though we end up peering at everything through a screen of steam.

"A fear of the unknown must not set boundaries for our lives. An overweening desire for comfort must not inhibit our appetites for danger." –Eugene Peterson, *This Hallelujah Banquet*

That much confessed, we're not dampened in the least. Our joy in this journey of exploration hasn't faded with the sun. We circle the *plaza* several times just to take another look at the towering cathedral decorated in birthday-cake colors. We discover an alluring restaurant called El Pomodoro. Italian, in Chiloé? (Out of many Chilotes' comfort zone, for sure.)

Then we park longingly in front of the closed gates of the fairgrounds for the traditional Customs Festival. Sigh, we'll need to return in the summer for that.

Moving on back downhill, we pass the provincial hospital, once so small even though it's the main medical facility for the archipelago. It has grown to occupy several blocks. We sweep around twice, gawking through a soup of car exhaust and rain. I imagine all my story characters gathered here at the climax of *The Sea-Silk Banner* (the series First Mate's Log #3).

Fog Magic

I ask my husband to head to the port area at the foot of Blanco Street. Here the Naval Administration building, the island base of the Chilean Armada, unpredictably depresses me. Though I never expected grand, its cold-shoulder entrance almost stings. Is it the steely-stern atmosphere, the leaden fiord behind blackened shingles, or maybe the renewed downpour that thrust me out of my comfort zone now?

With regret, I decide I may stick with my hazier memories for this story setting. In *The Seahorse Patrol* (First Mate's Log #1), my imagination conjures the magic of a naval reception, vivid and powerful, from a mere scrap of canvas and a glint of brass. Part of transforming our ordinary world, right?

On spur of the moment, we wind into the nearby souvenir market. Bypassing the outdoor stalls, we find the day's damp chill has penetrated the interior too, with all the doorways open. I look for ceramics or tins for my collections, but that's not Chiloé. The place is packed and stacked with wool items—sweaters, hats, ponchos, and rugs—and smells of sheep and woods and fried *sopaipilla* biscuits.

So I settle for a handknit hen for my kitchen shelf and a little knit doll magnet for the fridge. For my daughters, magnets made of cedar sticks and sand in the shape of *palafitos* (shacks-on-stilts). Nothing sophisticated, but they will remind the girls of the comfort of home. I wish I could locate a carved-apple doll like I once saw at a museum shop and featured in *The Seahorse Patrol*. Some things you have to snatch up in the right place at the right time, I guess.

Which is exactly what I realize as we approach the doors of Restaurant El Sacho for our customary anniversary lunch.

Noon Blues

It's closed! And then we remember, it's always closed on Mondays; Sundays are their big day. What a bitter disappointment for us. But we're not discouraged yet, just nudged unexpectedly out of our comfort zone. Don't we all sometimes resist going off script, avoid the detours—the bumpy ride and lumpy seats?

Occasionally, though, we need to have even our best routines shaken up a bit. My husband encourages me with the idea of discovering a new spot to celebrate, though he's less keen on spaghetti than I am.

"Marry someone who is a home and an adventure all at once." –Anonymous

Another place we check out along the waterfront is also closed for the season. But as we rumble once again past the unwelcoming naval headquarters, we notice a sort of combination *palafito* and *fogón*—a roofed, and in this case, enclosed firepit-style building. A gazebo on stilts over the water.

Immediately we hustle through the drenching shower into Restaurant Octavio. It's rustic but big, with soaring wood ceilings and plenty of tables. And *warm*. We cuddle up near the Bosca stove, its "slow combustion" presently roaring at top speed.

So our original frustration becomes a memorable *fiesta* along the Chilote seaside. Out of the comfort zone, we open new doors, admire different sights, embrace a change of menu. Ahem, well, *I* try exquisite crepes of crab Florentine. My husband steps out of the steak-eggs-and-onions box with round chips instead of fries. The waitress equals our friends at El Sacho for cheerful attention.

Octavio interrupts our careful plans for the day, breaks our familiar habits. We throw our ideas of comfort away as we head south out of town toward our next destination. Instead, we'll stop wherever we feel curiosity or inspiration. It's the best road to growth, after all.

Afternoon Showers

Our first unscheduled stop is Chonchi. We spent Saturday night just outside of this town, without seeing it. Remember, I folded Chonchi into Rilán to come up with the island village of Trilán for my First Mate's Log series.

Chonchi's a charmingly shabby town built on three levels, reminding me a bit of the country's major port of Valparaíso. So much wasted potential that I think about sending the character Valeria Serrano in to renovate this historic gem.

Suddenly we recall the old woman from Chonchi who used to squat outside the hardware store halfway down Blanco in Castro, selling plastic bags of *roscas*. In most of Chile, *roscas* are a version of donuts, but Chonchi *roscas* are donut-shaped semi-edibles drier than sawdust and more tasteless than soda crackers. At least, to my husband and me. Our kids gobbled them up, perhaps because that was their only snack during our busy mornings of errands.

Now we duck through the drippy doors into the town market to buy some *roscas* for the girls back home. Because this unique treat hails only from Chonchi. Like *licor de oro*, as we're reminded while inside the market, surrounded by golden bottles of every imaginable size. "Gold liqueur" may be flavored with saffron and lemon peel, but it's made of curdled milk. And it may get showcased in Turistel guides and TV documentaries too, but I've never seen real Chilotes actually drink the stuff.

Back on the highway, we turn off toward the west coast of Grand Chiloé, gliding along what's now a "comfort zone." The newly paved road to Cucao National Park hardly holds the shadow of a memory of the pot-holed wilderness track of our first drive out here many years ago.

But a misty jungle of thick green highlands still hedges the road, with the addition of scattered houses sporting satellite dishes and late-model vehicles parked in the driveways.

Dusky Dreams

We wind along the fog-banked shores of the Twin Lakes and come to what used to be the hamlet of Huillinco, nestled near the narrow strait between the lakes. This former widening of the road, strung with a few humble homes, figures in *The Seagull Operation* (First Mate's Log #2) as the crossfire setting of a civil war.

The character Melissa Travis, now a young adult, muses as she works in a makeshift field hospital, light years from her comfort zone:

> *"Could I ever fit into this strange world? Would love*
> *be enough when the initial exhilaration waned, when*
> *the rockets and sparklers fizzled? When life in Chiloé*
> *was just hard and routine and routinely hard? Maybe*
> *I should stick to the safe and familiar, the comfortable*

and—well, if not easy—at least, possible. I wasn't like
(others). I couldn't save the world if I tried."

You can't help everybody, she thinks. So often, I fret over
these same doubts. And answer myself as Melissa's sister
Linda does: *"No, you can't. But it makes a very big difference to*
the few you do help."

Something—someone—has made a difference here in
Huillinco, because it's become a proper village rather than an
overgrown intersection. I'm impressed by the transformation
that's taken place. Despite the curtains of rain, it feels so much
bigger and brighter than before. I take lots of pictures of the
medical *posta*, the two-story school, the firefighters' station.

Not much farther down the road lies Cucao, which also
plays a part in First Mate's Log. Cucao used to be the larger
community, but today it strikes me as stunted compared to
Huillinco. In a wooly white wrap of low-brushing cloud, we
bump along the muddy paths that pass for streets, find the
tiny school, the church, a few shops, and then cross the impos-
ing suspension bridge.

Evening Dew

A river, the outlet from the lake, runs through a sort of marshy
delta to the Pacific (where Huenchula, mother of the Chilote
"Little Mermaid," grew up). A Chilote version of the Golden
Gate Bridge sways over the river and connects the village with
the national park's main entrance. It's more silver-gray than
golden today, though. We drive into the west, where the sun is
setting behind a gauzy veil at the edge of the earth.

Within a few meters, we locate our headquarters for the next two days. The Palafito Cucao Hostel, another house-on-stilts at the water's edge, is a black shingle-clad "green" heaven. A spicy aroma of wood pervades and caresses the senses as soon as we enter.

We're expected to perch on a split-log bench in the entry hall, remove our shoes or boots, and don a pair of pigskin-soled knit slippers. I always thought those were just for tourist show, since you can skate on a lot more than ice on many Chilote floors. These are undeniably spotless, however. Though still cold at the end of September.

Our beautiful wooden box of a room looks like a nature refuge imported from a forest glen. Every surface is buffed to an opaque glow, but never painted, waxed, or varnished. Raw sheep's-wool blankets and throws cover the bed. Furnishings like abalone-shell soap dishes, braided-reed lampshades, and branches for towel bars surprise us. The absence of a TV doesn't.

We're threatened not to flush the T.P. (Talk about out of your comfort zone!) I try to remember to comply, but I'm tempted to wonder how it could possibly be more ecological to cart to a landfill or burn?

Just Before Dark

It's tea time, but we take a quick stroll on the boardwalk terrace. Rain-beaded white callas grow in thickets along the woven fences, like Easter lilies surviving and thriving outside the greenhouse. We smile at the rustic jacuzzi in a gigantic wooden rain barrel and regret we didn't book it. Too late now to heat it, but the contrast of sauna water and glacial air would have steamrolled us out of our comfort zone.

> *"Gratitude bestows reverence, allowing us to encounter everyday epiphanies, those transcendent moments of awe that change forever how we experience life and the world."* –John Milton

We fix our own supper and enjoy coffee, sandwiches, and donuts (not *roscas!*) at one of the indoor picnic tables adorned with driftwood sculptures. Happy anniversary. How far we've traveled from our comfort zone tonight. And how grateful for the ordinary epiphanies of the day.

Both of us have spent our lives pushed and pulled and prodded out of our comfort zone. Whether we've changed the world, we ourselves have changed and grown.

So that now we more often chose to move out of character, break the mold, rattle the status quo. Engaging with a new world means stepping through the door into the unknown.

And who knows what a difference that may make light years from here and millennia from now?

The Great Shapeshifter

The name of the Chiloé Islands' legendary ghost ship, the *Caleuche*, literally means "shapeshifter." It derives from the Huilliche words, *caleutún*, meaning "to change condition," and *che*, "people." Possibly chosen because of the ship's many transformations, the name could also refer to the changes in its crew from dead to alive, from torment to bliss, from scenes of disaster to visions of rapture.

The mythical "shapeshifter" remains a popular theme and character in modern literature. Witness movie phenomena such as the vampires, werewolves, and even all the superheroes. *Dr. Jekyll and Mr. Hyde, The Invisible Man. Twilight*, and the *Transformers*.

The Latin prefix *trans* means "across, beyond, on the other side." So transformation lies on the other side of a change of form. The concept of transformation within the context of a character arc constitutes one of the principal elements of any good story. Learning to change is so important that I return to the theme again and again. Are you a transformer? Have you encountered the Great Shapeshifter?

Because He can change everything. He can shift the shape of your life's craft from storm-buffeted to blessed.

What can we discover about transformation from the shapeshifter ship *Caleuche* of Chilote mythology?

Once Upon a Foggy Night

Some logical mythographers link the *Caleuche* with the Dutch pirate ship *El Calanche*, captained by Vincent Vaneucht, which once wandered about the myriad waterways of the archipelago and finally disappeared without a trace. The lost ship's treasure lies buried on some forgotten Chilote coast.

However, most islanders (at least pretend to) believe the *Caleuche* is a magic ship, a phantom ship sometimes said to be skippered by El Millalobo himself, the golden sea lion King of the Seas. It navigates the ocean depths as well as the surface, appearing with relative frequency in the channels of Chiloé.

But never, oh no, never in the full light of day.

Beware the tranquil nights, when the *Caleuche* materializes out of the swirling mist. From a distance, it looks like a great galleon of old, its aged sails shredded and draping from the masts like ragged reeds. A profusion of multicolored illumination creates a brilliant glow that highlights the ghost ship as it moves toward you at great speed.

Closer up… You may never glimpse the crew. The wooden deck's clear, but the ship rocks and shakes. You'll realize they're enjoying a rollicking good party below decks. It's said the *Caleuche* has a ballroom and an orchestra of flutes, horns, whistles, and many other mysterious instruments aboard. Music of extraordinary beauty and harmony floats from the interior on trails of mist.

And then… As unexpectedly as it appeared, the shapeshifter ship vanishes, erased by the dense fog flowing from the coasts. Almost instantly invisible. All that's left of this impressive "vision of rapture" is the echo of a captivating melody.

And perhaps the strange and hair-raising clank of anchor chains hauled up and dragged across the deck.

The Salvation of Shipwrecked Sailors

You can attempt to chase the *Caleuche*, of course, but you'll never catch her. Pursuit—whether motivated by curiosity, greed, or revenge—only causes the Shapeshifter to transform into a dolphin or a heavy trunk of cypress floating on the waves. The crew may turn into slippery sea lions reclining along the shore.

Not that Captain Millalobo's craft avoids human contact, necessarily. But it's on his terms. During her voyages around the channels and islands, the *Caleuche* helps many friendly ships to survive the fierce storms, conducting them to safe ports or even towing them... at speeds which, according to the storytellers, cannot be explained apart from magic.

But take care not to get too close without an invitation, no matter how alluring the call of the boisterous band music. You might end up misled into foundering on a rocky reef.

Because the *Caleuche* recruits crew members from two main classes of sailors. Some are the "blessed," those shipwreck victims rescued and transported (shanghaied, some might suggest) by El Millalobo's favorite daughter, La Pincoya, and her siblings. The moment their cadavers land on the deck of the *Caleuche*, they revive to a new life of eternal bliss in the great ever-after.

The Rendezvous of the "Righteous"

Or not. Chiloé's guild of witches' covens, the self-styled Righteous Province, comprise the second class of crew in *Caleuche* mythology. It's an ongoing debate whether their existence is a complete tall tale or has some basis in truth.

Destiny at Dolphin Bay focuses on unraveling the myth. Is the *Caleuche* a mysterious marine mirage? Or a fearful apparition piloted by the ghosts of pirates and conquistadores? The spectacle inspires awe, for sure. But also provokes terror in its victims.

Is it real? Common sense tells you no, of course not. Yet… who listens to logic alone in the fog after dark?

Chilote witches are said to possess the ability to fly, either through shapeshifting into a bird or by wearing a *macuñ*, a sort of magic flight jacket (yeah, I know, sounds like sci-fi). But they can only travel out to the *Caleuche* mounted on the bouncy flank of a Caballo Marino. This is no ordinary seahorse, but a mythological creature kept to serve the *machis*.

The witches sometimes maintain service agreements of their own, contracts called *pautos*, with ambitious shopkeepers who've become greedy enough to make a pact with the devil. In Chiloé, if you meet a man who's fast-tracked to the top of his profession, become rich within a short time, or started out with just a few articles of stock and now owns a grand commercial establishment… Well, all the neighbors will swear that the *Caleuche* frequently anchors in the cove in front of his house or below his *palafito* (shack-on-stilts), because they've heard the resounding thud of chains just before dawn.

The Longing for Everlasting Life

People claim that the shapeshifter ship and her crew of magic-artists supply these businesspeople with an abundance of goods. In return for...? Of course, there's a price attached to this sudden, amazing prosperity.

Returning to the lucky sailors transported to an eternal cruise through the seas of Chiloé, you have to wonder at the practical appeal of such an endless "undead" existence. Even the fabulous wealth and beauty wouldn't raise "halfway home" to the level of rapture in my book.

Once a year, the story goes, *Caleuche* crew members can obtain leave from their skipper for a brief furlough to visit their grieving families. Thus, they have the opportunity to bring them comfort and even economic aid. Sounds good, unless the families are freaked out by the appearance of spooks from the phantom ship.

Sometimes, these ghostly visitations continue year after year. In other cases, they never occur again—this most frequently, when the deceased returns to soothe his supposedly inconsolable widow, only to find her in the arms of another husband!

This aspect of the intriguing and complex legend of the *Caleuche* relates to the belief of almost every people group on Earth in a future destination where, when we arrive beyond the portals of death, we find a home and live happily forever, instead of simply disappearing, digested by worms and barnacles.

Perhaps, then, this part of (pagan) Chilote mythology corresponds to the sacred lake of the Egyptians, the nirvana of the Buddhists, and the paradise of the Muslims and Jews, etc.

It seems appropriate that a marine people such as the Chilotes might imagine the deck of a ship as the ideal eternal resting place beyond the grave.

The Hope of a Happy Hereafter

So the innate fear of death, more or less constant for those who work in or near deep and treacherous waters, is transposed into a great consolation. The prospect of ultimate rescue by the *Caleuche*, with the guarantee of material spoils and a superior life, bolsters the seamen. Their families are encouraged with the hope of seeing lost loved ones again, even as elusive spirit beings.

Folklorists trace the origin of the *Caleuche* myth to common mirage phenomena which lends itself to multiple interpretations in the different cultural contexts of the world. Here, for me, lies life's fundamental yearning: For meaning which death cannot destroy.

We long to pass from this place of toil and trouble, misunderstanding and miscarried justice, to the land where happiness and wholeness are no hallucination. Where only those who wear the robes of Jesus's true righteousness will win rewards.

> *"Behold, I tell you a mystery; we will not all sleep, but*
> *we will all be changed…and this mortal must put on*
> *immortality."* –St. Paul,
> I Corinthians 15:51-53, NASB

The heaven we Christians anticipate is no myth, but a blessed assurance. Most of us will gain it through the transformation of death (rather than rapture) into never-ending life by the transcendent power of the death and resurrection of Jesus Christ. *"This hope we have as an anchor of the soul, a hope both sure and steadfast"* (Heb. 6:19, NASB).

Nevertheless, the central theme of the Christian gospel is life, not death. Love, not luck. Grace, not gold. It's as much about a transformed today as it is about a transformed tomorrow.

The Truth About Transformation

Like the translation through death to eternity, we cannot be transmuted to a better life without changing form. And without Jesus, the Great Shapeshifter, we seldom change.

Now, I realize that the Almighty God-who-became-flesh hardly resembles the typical storybook shapeshifting character, pack-oriented and fantastical if not downright diabolical. Jesus is always good, and He is *"the same yesterday and today and forever"* (Heb. 13:8, NASB). Unlike the *Caleuche*, Jesus never changes.

But like the *Caleuche*, He changes others. He shape-shifts *us*.

We need the changing. And honestly, we *want* transformation into something more and better. But we want it to happen like magic. We don't want it to cost or to hurt. No painful valleys or frightening storms.

I admit I don't want to suffer the tearing off of my old dragon skin (as in C. S. Lewis's *The Voyage of the Dawn Treader*). I dread giving up my cherished self and letting God shape me into His image. But I've discovered you have to die before you can live.

Mere learning, wishing, and desiring won't transform you and me. But shaping ourselves around the Truth will. To shift our thinking, we need to walk as much as we talk, and work more than we weep. It's not enough to pray—we must plan and prepare. And maybe perspire. Imagine, dream, yes, but also do. Don't just evaluate, encourage. Don't just reach, stretch.

It doesn't always follow that we practice what we preach or heed the advice we dispense. Sometimes we limp along, wearing just one shoe of the pair marked Faith and Obedience. But Jesus said, *"If you know these things, you are blessed if you do them"* (Jn. 13:17, NASB).

Know...and do. Be informed, then transformed. And you'll be blessed.

Someday, beyond death, on the other shore, the myth of change will become reality. The tale of the Great Shapeshifter of our souls will turn out to be the truest and best story ever told.

Get Lost in a Good Way

On Day 5 of our Return to Chiloé trip, we're so far from civilization that we have practically no cell phone coverage and we had to bring *cash* to pay for our lodging at the Palafito Cucao. Since we plan to stay two nights here, we decide to forget the world today and just get lost …in a good way, of course.

"The only people who ever get anyplace interesting are the people who get lost." –Henry David Thoreau

Last evening we did a quick trundle around the Pacific coastal hamlet of Cucao, crossed the rather impressive suspension bridge, and arrived just outside the entrance to Cucao National Park. Now, we take a leisurely morning. In the rustic dining room of the hostel—all wood and natural décor—the cook serves us *café con leche*, a *paila* (small double-handled pan) of hot scrambled eggs, and of course, homemade bread. She turns out to be a Huilliche (native Chilote) woman. Though reserved as most Chilotes, over breakfast she willingly answers our questions about her tribal leadership and life in the area.

I'm reminded that the environs of Cucao play an important role throughout *The Seagull Operation* (First Mate's Log #2), as the site of a major skirmish of the "insurrection" I portrayed in that book. Little did I imagine when I wrote it that similar tensions would spring to all-too-real life a few years later in the current quasi-civil war of Chile's Araucanía Region.

West Side Story

By far, the great majority of the scattered islands and island groups of the Archipelago of Chiloé lie off the eastern coast of the Big Island. We spent most of our eight years in Chiloé in and around the rickety roads and stormy seas of that more populated east side.

The west side's another story. It's bleak, desolate, remote enough to disappear in. Or certainly used to be. As we rumble back across the bridge to again view the tiny village that appears in *The Seahorse Patrol* and *Swan Song*, I can't help remembering my first visit here in April (mid-fall) of 1987. Thirty years have produced a lot of changes.

For one thing, no town to speak of existed in those days. At least, that I noticed, though there must have been a smattering of homes because the site is ancient. The military government had created and marked out the national park in 1982, but the area was still perfectly primeval and practically unknown in '87.

It took a well-read tourist or a keen back-to-nature type to hear about Cucao in those early years. Which I guess our visiting friends were. They wanted to go, so we packed up the children and headed out on an exploration excursion.

We had only a small, capped pick-up. I don't know how our guests stood the three-hour drive from Dalcahue, freezing in the unlined truck bed, rattling along that pot-holed dirt road. Even inside in the cab, it seemed like torture, a wet, miserable day of grinding through highland hedges that hovered and menaced like dark giants over the road.

When we finally arrived at our destination on the west coast, it was late afternoon…

On the Wild Side

We slogged through foggy woods to the shore. But the day's thin light had nearly seeped into the horizon by the time we reached the Pacific. All I remember is cold and clammy blackness, and it's a miracle we didn't get lost on the hike back. No wonder we scurried home to hot soup and fireside.

That year, I'd just started dreaming and sketching the bones of my first book, *Destiny at Dolphin Bay*. Apparently, the trip to Cucao at that point didn't strike me enough to make it into the first trilogy.

However, in the summer of 1995, we visited again, and again with family and friends. And *this* time I fell under the spell of Cucao's mysterious allure. The wilderness park of coastal dunes, Valdivian rainforest, swamps, and peat bogs, had become *the* cool place to go for local students in the '90's. They blazed the trails on weekend campouts.

We barbecued on a wide strip of marshy riverbank where dozens of other visitors were also setting up rustic picnics. Then we hiked again to the shore, tramping through powdery, ankle-deep sand that coated our shoes with dust. At the edge of the ocean, on a long tidal flat, we adults snoozed among the dunes while the five kids roamed the shell-studded beach. They picked up bags of clamshells which they sold as souvenirs for months to come in our more northern inland city.

The tale sounds humble in the retelling. But the enchanting, light-filled spot so captured the imagination of one of my daughters that, years later, she painted herself in the scene from a photo: Wandering in a ruffly ankle-length dress instead of jeans, lady of the last undiscovered wilderness shore.

Side Trips

Today, it's our third trek back. Cucao National Park is now a popular ecotourist destination because of the amazing biodiversity of its nearly untouched Valdivian temperate rainforests and colonies of sea lions. We're excited about getting lost on a forest adventure.

But first, lunch. We've seen a couple of hole-in-the-wall possibilities along the muddy roadside and stop at a picturesque place called El Fogón de Cucao. A *fogón* is a glorified firepit, but this one must be the most appealing we've ever encountered. Inside, it's painted full-circle with murals depicting Chilote life and still decked with flag garlands and red-white-and-blue streamers from the September 18th patriotic holiday of early spring.

The friendly woman who waits on us talks so much we wonder if she can be a true Chilote. But what could be more back-to-our-roots Chilote than boiled potatoes, smoked pork, and garden lettuce? Answer: Nothing!

While we eat, we glimpse across the road a large two-story house with several half-moon balconies. Despite the whimsical architecture, it looks like it grew up there by itself and belongs to the landscape. I know I'm going to incorporate it into a book someday.

And I determine to stay there on my next visit to Chiloé. I believe it's called Darwin Stop, after the explorer/naturalist who visited Chiloé on his round-the-world voyage aboard the HMS *Beagle* in the 1830's. That detail, too, has made its way into my stories (such as *Legacy of the Linnebrink Light*).

Side Roads

First pause on our afternoon walk: the interpretive center run by CONAF rangers, Chile's Forestry Service which now administers the national parks. We buy Chilote flora and fauna posters to display in our home for years to come. For now, they fit carefully into my husband's backpack.

In a park this big and time this short, it's impossible to reach the sea lion rookery on the islet Metalqui, the exquisite beach at Cole-Cole, or the Chepu River area in the north. We stick to getting lost on El Tepual Loop, which we've hiked before.

But this time, it seems longer and wider, with plenty of signposts and lookouts, as well as miles of boardwalk covered with fishing nets to safeguard against the slippery wood. None of that was here before, on this wilder, wetter side of Chiloé. The annual rainfall may average 3,000+ mm a year. Though it's not pouring today, it's overcast and damp. Typical weather for Chiloé. Home sweet home.

Old-growth Valdivian rainforests such as the one we're roaming through are made up of perennial trees, shrubs, and climbing vines. They tend to form layered canopies with a dense undergrowth consisting of (for example): *Fitzroya alerce* (a cedar similar to the giant sequoia), *Nothofagus* (evergreen southern beech), *arrayán* (Chilean myrtle), *quila* (Chilean bamboo), *nalca* (Chilean rhubarb), numerous ferns and, of course, *tepa*. A *tepual* is a woods of *tepa* trees, a type of laurel.

By the Wayside

Along the way, we snap the forest photo I later decide will make a tantalizing book cover someday. When we finally approach the shore, it tumbles on forever in dunes and beach scrub before meeting the slate-blue ocean. For a place I've only visited a few times, it's so familiar that I can't get lost.

This I recognize as the setting of a pivotal scene in *The Seahorse Patrol*. I can't help recalling the characters Nicolás and Melissa's hiking date here and their meeting with the Villegas family, who live past the CIDER sign. Then there's a barge collision on the river and later a bombardment. No more spoilers!

Back at the hostel after our hike, my husband takes a nap. But I'm too lost in fascination with the rapidly changing sunset views from our window. I keep taking pictures but can't capture the strange back-lit gloaming. Below our small balcony, the silver-blue inlet shimmers, speckled with the tips of cranberry-colored reeds. Across in the village, the church tower soars stark against a watercolor sky, now petal-pink, now pewter.

Though we didn't travel far today, it feels like we've visited a forgotten world... Lost in that good way where your heart rewinds to fleeting memories of old friends from far and near. We've revisited pieces of our past and found fragments of the future, too.

It's dusk now. We're running out of snacks, so tonight's tea will be…well, not skimpy, but a little boring. Tomorrow, we'll find our way back to the highway—and home.

The Fear of Change

Reading through Dr. Bernardo Quintana's mythology treatise, *Chiloé Mitológico*, I'm struck once again by the background motivation of *fear* in so many of the rites and rituals, tall tales and strictly timed tasks. Fear of the spirits and the sickness they cause. Terror of darkness and death and the dead, as manifested in the story of the phantom ship, *Caleuche*. Fear of meager harvests and scarce fishing. And clearly, the fear of change and of lack and of the unknown.

The story of the *Caleuche* is one of the most intriguing and well-known of the many legends of Chile's Chiloé Islands. You may remember that the ship's name means "shapeshifter." It's not only capable of self-transformation from magnificent galleon to dolphin or dead tree trunk, it also can resurrect shipwreck victims and alter any islander's fortunes at whim.

Despite the positive aspect of some of these shapeshifts, few Chilotes desire to run into the *Caleuche* on a night of drifting fog. Would you? Me neither. Because it means you'd either be tottering on the brink of death or toying with mysterious powers beyond logical comprehension.

"The fear of man brings a snare... The fear of the Lord is beginning of wisdom..." –Prov. 29:25, 1:7 (NASB)

Some fears, no doubt, are right and reasonable, quite justifiable. Just not the fear of change.

Covenant of the Covetous

So what price does the witch-crew of the *Caleuche* put on their pact to upgrade an islander's prosperity? (Most of us never fear a change in fortunes for the better, only for the worse!) Part of this deal with the devil includes lavish on-demand entertainment of the ship's crew, in return for plenty of contraband goods.

When the *Caleuche* appears in front of a "partner" family's home, it's not always to drop off supplies. Every once in a while, the crew takes shore leave to have a bit of fun. Their hosts seem delighted to show them more than even customary Chilote hospitality. After the fiesta of abundant feasting and drinking concludes at dawn, the happy Caleuchans board their invisible ship again and lift anchors.

All the neighbors suspect that "Pepe Pérez" owes his economic success to a secret alliance with the *Caleuche*'s enchanted crew. Some people may even contend they *know* it for a fact because they've heard the all-night parties. Protected and provided for by powerful friends, naturally Pepe's obligated to pay up from time to time.

On the other hand, "Juan Jaque's" misery and woe may stem from some offense against El Millalobo, the Lord of the Seas. Instead of an exchange of favors between business associates, his visit from the *Caleuche* may signify something far more ominous. Such as punishment imposed for some act the captain and crew consider a crime.

They say a guy named José Huala, from the hamlet of Coñab (where we used to drive by weekly), once used explosives to fish. For this scandalous misdeed, he was compelled to the end of his days to hold big bashes for the *Caleuche*'s crew. The enormous expenses incurred occasioned great poverty to the unfortunate Huala.

Or... Curse of the Condemned

However, his sentence was mild compared to the case of Pancho Calhuante of the village of Matao. One night, while fishing near a rocky beach, he glimpsed a sea lioness nursing her young. He crept up on them and brutally whacked both mother and baby with an oar, killing the little one, which he dragged home to exploit for the oil of its blubber.

A short distance out to sea from Calhuante's front door, the wounded mother mourned the loss of her baby. On the fourth day after the attack, three sailors claiming to belong to the crew of the *Caleuche* suddenly arrived on his doorstep and announced that the fate of Calhuante's eldest son would mirror that of the baby sea lion. Sure enough, the child died a few days later.

Some folks insist you'd best not fish at all, or even dig shellfish, on those spooky foggy nights. Or you run the risk that the *Caleuche* may snatch you for her crew. All debts to the sea must be paid. A bitter lesson for those who dread poverty too much to show pity, who fear losing profit more than wrongdoing.

So these are the voyages of the shapeshifter ship *Caleuche*, on her continuing mission to explore the seas, supervise all its lifeforms, safeguard the next generation… Captain Millalobo takes his job even more seriously than Jean-Luc Picard.

Most folklorists see different angles to the *Caleuche* mythology. The care of marine life, of course, reflects the concern of all primitive peoples for plant and animal fertility and the bounty of annual harvests. As well as the modern preoccupation with global ecology and stewardship of the earth. The collecting of cadavers at sea, along with the reward or punishment according to works, recalls the future resurrection of the "just" and the "damned" in Christian theology.

Consternation in the Cove

These days, the legend of the *Caleuche* pops up most often in island humor. During our decade in Chiloé, we once experienced several months of rationed electricity when three of the four underwater electric cables to the island were damaged. Inexplicable? A ship had anchored too close to the cables, the power company conjectured.

Claro que sí-po. "Yeah, right." Our Chilote friends smirked. "It must have been the *Caleuche*."

In *Destiny at Dolphin Bay*, two harmless Chilote fishermen encounter a counterfeit apparition of the *Caleuche* and flee in panic. Tragedy ensues. Jaime and Lucho, the unlucky victims of a cruel and elaborate hoax, never view the crew of the *Caleuche* as benevolent rescuers (like La Pincoya and her siblings). Instead, their meeting with the ghost ship fills them with terror of the retribution of evil witches, meted out for some arbitrary offense.

In reality, they've become the brunt of a villain's fiendish greed (or jealousy or revenge, as in many stories). The old fear of diabolical spirits binds them under the control of defeated enemies and toothless snakes. Blinds them to the new truth of freedom from sin and death and hell. The new freedom from fear.

> *"A mind that is stretched by a new experience*
> *can never go back to its old dimensions."*
> –Oliver Wendell Holmes, Jr.

For some of these Chilote folks, the good news of rescue by Jesus provokes more fear of change than desire for a transformed life. While I do see a lot of change for change's sake these days, I remind myself that sometimes my fear of change merely equals a fear of the unknown.

But proceeding with thoughtful caution… Dear God, don't let my mind harden to cement or my heart turn into stone. I may (will!) grow older, but don't let me get set in my ways.

"Though the mills of God grind slowly, yet they grind exceeding small," wrote the poet Henry Wadsworth Longfellow. God is in the process of transforming hearts in this world, no matter how small and slow the changes seem.

He is the only One who can make things better. Let's not get twisted up with the fear of change. Can we choose the pain that renovation means, the work and effort and sacrifice it costs to become changed people?

> *"When the winds of change blow, some people build walls*
> *and others build windmills."* –Chinese proverb

For other Chilotes, the fresh air of the gospel wafts into their lives like a spring breeze from a brand-new world. They recognize that none of us live free of sorrow and hardship. This present world is no utopia of endless bliss.

Yet they've learned that the cheap spoils of the devil don't come at bargain prices, either. Clinging to their deeply entrenched customs and human concepts of the good life has never created a just society among them. The culture offers solidarity, conformity, even stability. But it never gives the gift of peace. And never erases their lurking fears.

"Even though I walk through the valley of the shadow of death, I fear no evil, for You are with me..."
–Psalm 23:4 (NASB)

Some, like the character Nicolás, come to see that righteousness and peace meet in Jesus alone. He steps up to challenge *"the futile way of life inherited from (our) forefathers"* (I Peter 1:18, NASB) and confront the false Righteous Province (the witch crew sailing the shapeshifting *Caleuche*) and their imitators.

Their external works not only lack the power to produce the internal transformation of a lost, frightened, and darkened soul. They also exacerbate the fear of change: One's fortunes might turn, all right. Things can always get worse, is the philosophy.

Replacing the Rags

Yet the Apostle Paul calls this vain thinking the *"empty deception"* of human traditions (Col. 2:8, NASB). And Nicolás, too, calls it as he sees it: *"It hardly matters whether you change religion or government or even your own habits."* Neither plastic surgery nor political upheaval will ever change the heart. Or the world.

And even less, catering parties for the Evil One in the hope of finding acceptance, approval, or financial assets.

In another story, a Chilean woman—a visitor to a certain island—relates her horror upon discovering that the ten-year-old grandson of a neighboring couple was experiencing chronic sexual abuse. The boy's young single mom had long since departed the island to escape her father (*her* abuser, as well).

But when this concerned woman approached local authorities—a teacher and a police officer—she was stopped cold. They begged her not to make a stink about the situation. *Please* not to upset the apple cart, not to disturb the unity of the island. Those well-meaning people sincerely believed it better to "leave it alone," or the family would lose their sole means of support and a "respectable" elder would lose face.

Better in the short term, maybe. But talk about the fear of change.

The attitude expressed seems to imply that we're locked into the way we are. That people, families, nations, *cannot* change.

Perhaps not. But I believe in a Rescuer who extends His hand while He rocks the boat and says, *"Behold, I am making all things new"* (Rev. 21:5, NASB).

Be a True Transformer

When, in the cultural narrative, an assault on a sea lion carries weightier consequences than abuse of a child, something's out of balance in our world. Is it kindness to rescue the dead but not the living? To fuss about funeral feasts instead of relief for the wretched and broken?

Or to watch vicious cycles of dysfunction drag on to the third and fourth generation…or *every* succeeding generation? How easily we human beings are tempted to tolerate the intolerable, slide into the mud of mediocrity, and embrace evil—but not the costly treasure of transformation.

"Transformation in the world happens when people are healed and start investing in other people."
–Michael W. Smith

You know I'm for enjoying stories. I'm a fiction writer and a fan of fairy tales and fantasy. Some stories may feature "good" wizards, but most of Chiloé's real *machis* scramble for influence and affluence, oppose God, and even impersonate Him in their locale.

In real life, you'll find me siding squarely with the True Story of the One who came to break all evil spells and shatter our petty status quo. He means to shift the shape of our jaded thinking to joy. *If* we will trade our frantic pursuit of health, wealth, and happiness for the Unchanging Savior who can change everything.

Let's lose our fear of change. Roll out of the ruts of routine.

And perhaps the fear of *not* changing, too. But that's a debate for another day.

"In the days (of God's King) may the righteous flourish, and peace abound, till the moon be no more! May he have dominion from sea to sea… May people blossom… (and) the whole earth be filled with his glory!"
(Ps. 72:7-8, 16, 19, ESV)

Blue Plate Special

Though it's rained nine-tenths of our time in Chiloé, I can tell this final day of our trip to the Chiloé Islands is going to be extra special from start to finish. What I notice most are dishes of comfort food and the color blue, so I think I'll call it the Day of the Blue Plate Special.

According to online sources, a blue-plate special is a low-priced meal, usually rotating daily, at diners and cafés in the United States and Canada. Though it dates to the late 1800's, the concept of classic-but-cheap food came to popularity during the 1920's through the 1950's. Today, the tradition is vanishing.

Sadly, because it's the ultimate combo of simple and simply yummy. The common made fit for a queen. A blue-plate special takes the ordinary and surprises and delights us with its awesome "extra" factor.

Into the Blue

We awaken at dawn. The early light glows misty blue over the water outside our little hostel balcony. The village of Cucao across the narrow river lies in a pearlescent bath of blue so ethereal it hurts the eyes to look. And look we'd better, for the scudding indigo clouds promise the clear weather won't hold out long today.

"Keep your face to the sunshine and you cannot see a shadow." –Helen Keller

So my husband and I breakfast quickly and get on the road. We have to catch a mid-afternoon plane out of Puerto Montt, at least four hours away counting the drive and ferry crossing back to the mainland. The road to Castro, the island's capital, skims along the edge of the Danube-blue Twin Lakes, through patches of velvet shadow and pools of silvery morning sunlight. Compared to our dreary drive out the day before yesterday, this trip is a once-in-a-blue-moon special.

The treat lasts only until we reach Castro. There, out of the blue, rain begins to splash down, heavy enough to confine us to the car while we make a final swing by the waterfront. The streets smell like fresh laundry. We pass the Blue Unicorn again, the emblematic hotel we've always wanted to stay at but haven't got to yet. Ironically, it's painted Pepto-Bismol pink.

We hit the road north toward the ferry in time to make a few stops along the way. First, Chilolac Dairy, another island icon. We pause to buy a kilo brick of nutty Gouda cheese. Oh, that stuff is delicious. I'm obsessed with it! At least, it isn't blue cheese.

Next, we detour into Ancud for a second breakfast at the Blue Galleon, which is neither blue nor a galleon, but rather a hotel/restaurant near the regional museum that my characters Melissa and Nicolás visit on one of their rare dates. The Blue Galleon's whimsical architecture sports canary yellow shingles, Pacific blue rooflines, and a high round tower.

True Blue

Inside, we sip our *café con leche*, enjoying the stone-flagged floors, buffed wood, and arched windows framing a scenic view of the colonial city's stunning harbor. A blue-plate special, for sure.

And what is it with blue today? We ask ourselves. What's so special about blue?

With such tried-and-true, calm-and-cool character, it shouldn't surprise us to learn that the color blue has the most universal appeal. It's the world's favorite color. Perhaps not everyone's, but I confess it's mine. What's not to love about the heavenly hues of sky and sea?

Blue is associated with serenity, sincerity, and creativity. And though it *can* symbolize depression and loneliness— you've heard of blue moods and baby blues—it also speaks to our intuition, inspiration, and imagination.

What would've become of Pinocchio without the Blue Fairy? Or Cinderella without her Príncipe Azul, the Spanish language's name for Prince Charming? The Blue Prince of the fairy tales presumably carries the "blue blood" of nobility. (Their skin was so fair, people said, that you could see their blue veins.) Or…he might literally wear blue, since blue pigment was scarce and expensive in the past. Only the wealthiest could afford it.

What a blessing these days when we can all manage a pair of blue jeans, that timeless fashion classic. In western cultures, blue is the color of faithfulness and trust, seen in the "something blue" of wedding traditions. And of responsibility and authority—think the blue power suit of corporate America.

Then you have blue eyes, blue hair (seen regularly on the Santiago subway), blue language (also *heard* on the *metro*), blue streaks, blueprints, and Bluenoses (those lucky enough to be born in Nova Scotia, like my oldest daughter). And we all can rejoice in our heritage on God's special and beautiful blue planet.

Plate Combinations

Blue pottery and porcelain, such as the type popularized by the Spode and Wedgwood china companies, feature among the most cherished in the world. During the Great Depression, inexpensive plates divided into separate sections like a cafeteria tray were manufactured in bulk. One historian mentions these plates were only available in blue and often decorated with the famous Blue Willow pattern. Therefore...the blue-plate special.

Before McDonald's and KFC, mid-century USA used to serve up a square meal with the fixin's for less than a dollar. Whatever was cheap and delicious turned up on the blackboard: hot roast beef sandwiches, fried chicken, fish and chips, turkey dinner with the works.

In my home area of Maine, you'd see meatloaf, macaroni and cheese, and chowder on the list. One summer during college, I worked at such a locally beloved watering hole and tucked into a BLT and a chocolate milkshake every day for lunch. Then there were...the pies! Nothing makes me drool like one of our graham cracker pies. (Maybe it's a Maine thing?)

The Blue Plate Special offered quintessential American comfort food. It evokes memories of happy, simpler times—home, Mom, and apple pie (or whatever kind *you* hanker for). Those wholesome, country-style dishes combined old-fashioned flavor with serious substance.

Nothing gourmet, but it was *good*. Never intended to wow, just quietly wonderful.

Here in Chile, before Telepizza and the food court at the mall, we were blessed with the marvelous *menú del día* at restaurants. The day's special always included bread with *pebre* salsa, soup or salad—or maybe both—and then… Bean-and-sausage casserole, *cazuela* stew, steak and eggs, flawless rice with fried fish… Dessert would follow: *flan* custard, pineapple ice cream, or poached pears, perhaps.

Plate Collections

As American diners discovered the novelty of salad bars, all-you-can-eat buffets, and ethnic fare, times they were a-changing. Doggy bags morphed into Styrofoam boxes. In Chile, we never did have those blue dishes, but the advent of bring-your-own-take-home-containers has also meant flimsy paper straws and balsawood cutlery in the interests of going green. Oh, give me that blue-plate special!

At home, I collect real plates (along with my legendary tins). Many *are* blue plates, gathered from travels near and far: Blue Willow from a delve into a New Brunswick antiques shop, Delft from Germany, Mexican ceramics from Chiapas, and a lozenge-shaped tile from the souk in Old City Jerusalem.

Some are truly special, such as my grandmother's home-town sesquicentennial souvenir plate featuring the red-brick library clocktower and the engraved copper plate inlaid with lapis lazuli stones—a twenty-fifth wedding anniversary gift.

Still others are as ordinary and lovely as daily bread and butter: The set assembled piece-by-piece from a Chilean supermarket. The green-tinted rooster plates and the hand-carved wooden fruit platter. The square plates with powder-blue hydrangeas that cheered me each morning after a miserable move. Hopeful flowers for a blue lady.

And of course, I hang the plate collection on the wall. How could I appreciate them stacked away in a cupboard?

After coffee at the Blue Galleon, we make yet another food detour, last stop before the ferry dock. Die Raucherkate (The Smokeshack) sells smoked salmon from behind the red-and-gray herringbone door of a rustic black barn. I assume the German farmers keep their own little fishery along the shore below the meadow. That salmon turns into superb homemade sushi later.

Special Surprises

To our disappointment, in mainland Puerto Montt the traffic snarls so thick in the downpour that we don't have time to drive out to the iconic fish market at Angelmo. Lunch there— classic *paila* (seafood in broth) or even a humungous *pulmay* (clambake-in-a-pot)—comes served in a clay bowl instead of a blue plate. I'll take it anyway! And I'd settle for plain steamed mussels with lemon, sigh…

But I realize it's not going to happen today. At the airport, we stuff down something forgettable and overpriced on a plastic plate while we wait for our flight home to the capital. Then the unforgettable happens, a triple special as the sun bursts forth in glory as it rarely does in southern Chile this time of year.

*"Into all our lives, in many simple, familiar, homely ways,
God infuses this element of joy from the surprises of life,
which unexpectedly brighten our days, and fill our eyes
with light."* –Samuel Longfellow

Outside the gate window, our LATAM Airbus sits on the wet tarmac. Not a blue plate, but it's a blue plane, and the sudden sunshine glitters off the red stripe and white star on the tail. Above, only the odd patch of cloud blemishes a now blazing blue sky. And into the blue juts the snow-cone peak of Volcán Calbuco with the icy clarity of a crystal pyramid. Though it's many kilometers away, it looks like it's suspended right above us.

Later I learn that Calbuco means "blue water" in Mapudungún. Naturally.

So like the blue plate special of the good old days, the final hours of our Return to Chiloé trip feature the perfectly ordinary turned oh-so-extraordinary.

When we arrive home in Santiago...

Vendors crowd the sidewalks and subway stations, hawking street food like *sopaipillas* (flat fried biscuits) and *empanadas* (savory turnovers) from handheld baskets and cardboard boxes. There might be a soccer game scheduled because carts and tray-stands choke the access to the stadium. Get your ham and cheese sandwiches! Or hot dogs heaped with avocado and sauerkraut.

These days in Chile, maybe it's deep-fried sushi handrolls. Whatever, it's their blue plate special.

Stay alert, the "Special" signs may turn up anywhere. Like Chiloé itself—and in most of our lives—the best things aren't the expensive, gilded, spectacular moments but the amazing taste and beauty of every day.

Desperate For Love

During a recent exercise in researching writing topics, I was challenged to type "Desperate for..." into my browser. What did I discover? People are desperate for attention, approval, and affluence (usually they call that last one "money" or "a loan.") Women are desperate for a miracle, a man, a baby, or a house. And some are desperate for the weekend... or—even— the presence of God (sometimes specifically "Jesus" or "the Holy Spirit").

Try "Desperate to..." and you'll find people all desperate to know, learn, do, buy, or sell something. Desperate to travel. To please someone. To lose weight fast. And again, to get married.

Bottom line, most people are longing for a love relationship of some kind. Searching for significance and concerned for the future.

"It is not weakness to desire love. The weakness is when we settle for less than love." –Crystalina Evert

In today's return to the mythology of Chiloé, I'll trace the tale of El Trauco, an ugly troll-like spirit creature considered the father of "natural" children. (A legal, though somewhat archaic, term in Chile, meaning "born out of wedlock." Does that make marriage an "unnatural" state?! I suppose we'd use the word "biological" today.)

Once Upon a Time in a Dark Wood…

El Trauco is depicted as a hideous little monster (about 80 cm or 2.5 ft. tall) who inhabits the woodlands near Chilote homes and wears a ragged suit and conical bonnet made of *quilineja*, the husk-like leaves of a creeping vine also used to fashion baskets and brooms. He speaks but in guttural grunts, and his legs end in simple stumps. But he has the strength of a giant, can fell any tree in three whacks of the stone axe he carries.

And he seems to entice young women in great numbers! Of course, to many girls the lurking shadow of El Trauco instills a disquieting worry of the unknown, a dread to avoid at all costs. Their mothers share this preoccupation, knowing full well the result of his mischief. Desperate to thwart any forest encounters, they rarely send girls of a certain age alone into the hills in search of herbs or firewood. Even the company of a little brother will caution and scare off El Trauco, who never accosts in the presence of witnesses.

Yet many women, young and old, who've "met" El Trauco will insist he's not so bad. Despite his rather repugnant looks, he awakens an irresistible sensual attraction and holds a searing grip on their thoughts. They struggle to get him out of their mind.

But El Trauco focuses all his attention on single women, especially the pretty and pleasing ones. He's not interested in married women (who might be unfaithful, but never with him). Ever alert, El Trauco spends most of the day hanging from the branch of a *tique* (large, tall tree) in wait for his "prey." Perhaps the anticipated object of his desire, or perhaps a mere passerby who catches his fancy.

Desperate for a Woman

Here she comes... When he glimpses from his high perch a solitary girl he wants, El Trauco drops rapidly to the ground for the "attack." With his axe, he strikes the *tique* trunk three such resounding blows that its echo seems to tumble all the trees.

The strange noise startles the girl. Before she has a chance to recover from her fright, the fascinating Trauco appears beside her. His axe twists into a hollow wooden cane called the Pahueldón. From this magic stick wafts a soft and sweet but powerful breath.

Helpless to resist the magnetic force of El Trauco's spell, the girl fixes her gaze on the sparkle of his penetrating, diabolic eyes and falls into the bushes in surrender at his feet. Oblivious, she sleeps peacefully and dreams of erotic love, while he proceeds to deflower his target.

If anyone bothers or interrupts him in the process, El Trauco is said to blow a curse on them. This *aire* may deform the unfortunate snoop or even kill him on the spot.

"All that is buried is not treasure." –Unknown

When night falls, El Trauco returns home to his grumpy and sterile wife, the formidable Fiura. The daughter of La Condená (a sort of goddess of vice), La Fiura barely minds his extramarital activities—she concentrates on the local men!

Desperate for a Story

Meanwhile, the girl awakens, confused and tearful. Whether minutes or hours have passed, she has no knowledge. She scrambles to her feet, shakes the dry *quilineja* leaves from her disheveled hair, shoves on her tangled clothing, and stumbles, half-dazed, in the direction of her home.

As time passes, the body of the girl possessed by El Trauco undergoes dramatic changes. She never tries to hide her pregnancy, since she feels that she is not a "sinner" but the victim of a supernatural being before whom, everyone knows, no single woman can stand.

In the old days, Chilotes tried numerous bizarre rituals to rid themselves of the presence of El Trauco. Sometimes, this "protection" worked. And sometimes, nothing and no one can stop him.

Nine months later the child of El Trauco is born. So linked to the fairy tales of island mythology, neither mother nor baby suffers any social disgrace due to their situation. No awkward questions, no pointed fingers or whispered names.

In general, all Chilote myths relate in some way to good or bad luck, death or life (fertility and sexuality). In the figure of the Trauco, *all* is sexual symbolism. This salacious troll creature corresponds to the vampire or incubus of European myths.

Desperate for a Man

The myth of the Trauco developed important implications, out of whatever moral necessities existed during earlier cultural periods. First, it acted as a defensive weapon, a brake, if you will, to the sexual impulse by inducing young women to conserve their virginity.

Then, after a done deal, the Trauco constituted a satisfactory excuse for a pregnant single woman. The tale portrayed the woman and child as innocents and permitted them to live in their rural society without the significant social stigma experienced in many places not so many years ago. Sadly in Chile, the child often received more of the brunt of illegitimacy than his mother, who sooner or later would marry and leave El Trauco's son behind with Grandma.

In *Pursuit of the Pudú Deer* (Desert Island Diaries #2), the character Melissa Travis's nemesis, Delicia, is pregnant. The kids in town say—with a snide grin—that she ran into El Trauco last summer. Because everyone's pretty sure the father of her baby is *not* the guy she's blaming. In fact, maybe she's La Fiura herself.

The Trauco tale is pretty much a worn-out joke in these modern times. But in those ultra-conservative, pre-divorce, pre-DNA days in Chile, men rarely acknowledged out-of-wedlock paternity. They might even be censured themselves if it were known publicly. False accusations abounded. Just not so much in Chiloé…

But the legend of El Trauco traces to more than just the hanky-panky of youthful passion. After all, those slip-ups were/are quickly fixed with shotgun weddings. In *Hope Chest*, I deal with a more sinister side of the Trauco myth.

Desperate for the Truth

In many instances, the skeletons in the closet wear the disguise of the Trauco. The truth is, we have married men and even relatives involved here. Rape, incest, adultery, and a web of seduction not always woven by the guys. Some young single girls made it almost a game to pursue the married men, especially those working away from home.

A dangerous gamble too, because the women—and children—always ended up paying the bill. Sometimes over and over. Desperate for love, or one of its many inferior substitutes…pleasure, popularity, validation, admiration? All fun until someone gets hurt. The amusing antics in the thicket seldom make it to the golden anniversary party.

Why did everyone cover so much up with an old story and a bitter laugh? Compassion, of course, for victimized girls— and even for faithful wives back tending the home fires and hoeing the potato patch.

But compassion gone wrong, I wonder? Never to expose wrongdoers leads to lots of new little Traucos keeping the generational wheel spinning.

God's grace is oh-so-much greater than all our sin, but many people don't want grace. Because it implies they *need* it. What's so bad about being good? Or pure? Because it might make someone feel they don't measure up?

Who does? I don't, and I mean that. I can't change the past, but I can be forgiven and change the future. Every day I chose a new beginning *"in paths of righteousness for His name's sake"* (Ps. 23:3, ESV).

And now we have bumped into the elephant in the room, and I doubt if I can get around it without stepping on somebody's toes: Why does the idea of righteousness—true right living—offend so? And should we follow my truth or your truth? Or…God's truth?

Desperate for Life

Let me confess I don't want anyone inspecting the closet of my heart either, but that doesn't mean it doesn't need occasional cleaning and ordering. Are my Christian values too black and white? Gray seems to be the fashionable shade these days. Are the lines of my (life)style too hard...or too soft? God keep me from choosing *anything*, whether old or new, just because it's trendy.

"Why fit in when you were born to stand out?"
–Dr. Seuss

Yeah, I know I'm kind of uncool. Believe me, I'm not steamrolling to scold, shame, or chastise my friends. But sometimes I just feel called to unmask that monster in the woods who disdains dignity and discipline and dismisses monogamous marriage as an "unnatural" restraint.

The robe of righteousness is costly. But you can squander a lot of your soul, too, in the search for a bright new soulmate under every tree. I'm not afraid to guard my treasures and lift up a beacon to beauty and purity. And shine a bit of light in the wilderness.

Most people wander along, desperate for life, liberty, and the pursuit of happiness, in the best way they know how. But behind that chasing of the wind often hides a fear of death.

How's that, you ask? Because we're desperate to be noticed, remembered, loved, appreciated, respected. We fear loss, pain, inferiority, disappointment, and defeat. We fear that our lives may turn out useless, meaningless, joyless.

Desperate for a Romance

Later in life—sometimes not so late—we fear sickness, loneliness, and unloveliness. Here's another dark path where El Trauco lurks and plays tricks on the mind. Chilote "spinsters" are convinced they must have at least a child or two so they won't be without caregivers in their old age. That social pressure to provide for themselves before it's too late overcomes even their fear of El Trauco.

As a writer, I was interested in Dorothy L. Sayers's take on the *"artificial happiness"* of some storybook characters in her exploration of Christian creativity, *The Mind of the Maker*. (Author of the Lord Peter Wimsey mysteries, Sayers was a contemporary of Agatha Christie and C. S. Lewis.)

She writes that when characters are *"...not permitted to suffer loss within their own microcosm, they have suffered irretrievable loss in the macrocosm."* In other words, if a writer doesn't allow her characters to suffer over the course of the plot, she actually kills the story. So true, right? Happy characters living perfect lives makes for a pretty flat storyline.

And our unwillingness to exercise restraint and limit our freedom even a little leads to big losses over the long haul of life. Never mind the stunted character growth.

"Make them laugh, make them cry, make them wait."
–Charles Dickens's rules for writers

Surprisingly, real romantic happiness involves an awful lot of dying to self. We resist that, reject it, fear it. But it's in all the best stories.

Snow White had to eat the poisoned apple to be awakened by the prince. Sleeping Beauty slumbered in a deathlike state for a hundred years. Cinderella endured a youth of drudgery. And think about *Beauty and the Beast*. In volunteering to save her father's life, she died a psychological death to hope, though it turned out better than beautiful.

In and outside of books, we're dying and desperate for love. Sometimes we think we're entitled to it. Yet we're totally confused about what it is and how to find it.

Happily Ever After

In these days of one-night stands and no-strings chain relationships, I'm often tempted to ignore the whole topic of love vs. lust in my writing. After all, who wants to be considered old-fashioned and outdated? The times endorse all kinds of sexual situations and set-ups, and in the era of pills and abortions and radically altered social mores, it's all much easier than inventing El Trauco.

In my browsing outside the "inspirational" genre, few characters even get married anymore, let alone wait for such an antiquated arrangement. Most of the romances feature forbidden relationships (what's "forbidden" today?) or fake engagements or re-encounters ten years after the baby. Or oh yes, the billionaire boss. (Fantasy, too!)

While it may present a challenge for the average writer to sell romance without sex, plenty of sex pops up without a pinch of romance. As a reader, I'm desperate for a "happily-ever-after" book that doesn't equate romance with bodice ripping and over-the-top sexual tension. Of course, we can go for the "sweet and clean" labels as opposed to erotica. But some of that tastes—dare I admit?—stale, saccharine, and boring.

How do I write God's truth in a world of honest emotions and hard choices? In life, there's such a thing as sweet spice and pure sex. But so often, instead of holding out for the best, we settle for the banal and barter the wonder of white-hot passion for cold, emotionless carnality.

God, make us desperate for true love, and nothing less. Make us desperate for You, and no lesser gods. *And make us wait.*

Back to the Beginning

This island is anything but posh or pretentious. But its aura grows on you. No one can leave here unchanged. Forever, my heart has ties to two worlds, my Gringoland birthplace and my adopted country. And let me narrow the focus to my first home in Chile, the microcosm of Chiloé.

Thanks for joining me on my odyssey of return. Why, after so many years, my connection here feels stronger than ever, I'm not sure. The bond remains unbroken. I came so young, and now...I'm not. But I'm still at home.

And yet not at home. Nothing is as it *seems*. I arrived, once upon a time, unaware of the currents writhing beneath the surface. But I learned far more than nuances of language, culture, and landscape. No longer ingenuous, I see with aching clarity the stumbling blocks, the rocky soil, the bleak emptiness, the pain and poverty that have no link to income.

But in the blinding fog, I find timely treasures of wisdom in this last corner of the earth, and the gold does not grow dim (Lam. 4:1, ESV). I've learned to weave the unholiest horror into poignant beauty through the magic of hope. I'm certain of what matters now.

Our choices matter. If God has appointed me—and you— to whatever pinpoint on the planet at this particular hour, then we're called to an awesome position. Who we are and what we do with the time and talents entrusted to us matter to God and to our generation. There's no such thing as ordinary or insignificant.

The truth matters. I suspect we've told and sold ourselves so many narratives, it's sometimes difficult to discern which reflect spiritual and eternal reality. But all the same, I will cling to the Word of God and what I know of His good heart, and not to my faithless feelings amid the fluctuations of circumstance. The God of truth reigns over my island kingdom, not my wobbly opinions.

"Here I stand. God help me. I can do no other."
—Martin Luther

Growth matters. That's the freshness that comes from sharpening dull minds, knocking on hard hearts, and breaking cultural barricades. It's transforming entire worldviews, and changing me before trying to change the world. It's learning to cope with change and also to trust when I see no change at all.

Joy matters. Finding the music in the endless rain, listening for the whisper of God's Spirit in the mist, is… well, a choice. When all seems drowned in despair and suffocated in suffering, I will sing the song of the ransomed captive, right now when everything seems wrong. I've found God not in the elegant literature of the elite but in the lonely coasts, barren hopes, and strange stories of Chiloé.

Love matters. Our God loves the world, but I'm sure He cares more for the people than the places. Of course, He beams on His magnificent creation, but He shines His greatest love on the unloved and unlovely of His fallen world. Oh God, let me find the beauty in ashes and mud and black bread and see the hearts inside the hovels.

"For it is one thing to see the land of peace from a wooded ridge...and another to tread the road that leads to it."
—St. Augustine, *Confessions*

Eternity matters. Life is a treasure to be spent not saved, savored not stored for later, invested not hoarded, because I'm already living in eternity. *"I've made the Lord my home..."* (Ps. 73: 28, MSG), and I plant myself firmly in a God who's sovereign in every situation and detail of life's design. While there's so much we don't see and may never know this side of heaven, I believe God has a plan that's much bigger than it sometimes looks.

When it feels like the clouds may never break, let alone the Enemy, that's when I trust the Sun and see the Invisible. Treasures hide along the darkest roads, where surely we'll meet the redeemed of Chiloé. Let's head toward the Light. And at the end of the journey is Home.

"Sing the Lord's praise from the end of the earth! You who go down to the sea, and all that is in it. You islands, and those who dwell on them... Let them declare His praise in the islands" (Is. 42:10, 12; NASB).

Acknowledgements

Today marks the fifth anniversary of our move to the port city of Coquimbo, at the edge of northern Chile's Atacama Desert. God has led me over long years in the wilderness from the storms of the Chiloé Islands to the droughts of the Elqui Valley. Thank you, Jesus, for streams in the desert this year and for the fields of *añañucas*, gravel-pit lilies, that flourished after the once-in-a-decade rain.

Flowers to Lisa Norman of Heart Ally Books for your dedication to excellence and frequent words of encouragement. Another bouquet goes to Colleen Shine Phillips, my writer friend, godly mentor, and faithful reader. An armful of southern mountain *copihues* to Christina Steward for all the Chile paintings, especially the one we chose for this book cover. And a bunch of tools for my husband, who builds our home while I fry the fish between finishing chapters.

"And what more shall I say? For time will fail me if I tell of... so great a cloud of witnesses surrounding us..." (Heb. 11:32; 12:1, NASB). Thanks to all the Gospel Mission of South America family (www.gmsa.org) who've blessed my life and cheered me on between Castro and Coquimbo. I'm especially grateful for the other writers among us and for long-time editor of the GMSA *Southern Sentinel*, Myra Shedd, who first inspired me to write about the ministry journey.

Besides those trailblazers mentioned in this book's dedication, I can't help but express my admiration for the many pioneer missionaries who served the gospel in Chiloé: Bernie and Margaret, Marvin and Peggy, Wendell and Grace, Katie, Pauline, Terry and Carol, Eric and Joy. (Those are some I know personally. Nell Festa Eggleston's book *Flying Coattails* highlights a number of others.) Surely they deserve a place on the Hebrews 11 Roll of Honor. And a big celebration clambake!

Thank you for joining me on this trip back in time. If you enjoyed *Return to Chiloé*, I'd be so appreciative if you could take a moment to leave a review wherever you purchased it and also on Goodreads or your other favorite book recommendation site. One of the greatest challenges authors face is enabling new readers to find their work. You can help by telling your friends and contacts.

Fast-forwarding to future projects, I'd love to invite those interested in further stories of how God works in my life in Chile to visit Seaglass Sagas at www.dianadelacruz.com. From time to time, I also share news about upcoming books. Let's meet at the beach and spin new legends of Chiloé.

About the Author

Diana Delacruz writes under a pen name to keep her ongoing missionary service low-key. In *Destiny at Dolphin Bay*, the opening book in the Desert Island Diaries, she draws on her almost 40 years of experience as a teacher, speaker, and writer in Chile. Diana and her husband work in the city of Coquimbo at present. They have three grown daughters and five grandchildren.

Diana grew up in the state of Maine and has never lived more than an hour or two distant from the ocean. You can learn more about Diana and her Seaglass Sagas at www.dianadelacruz.com.

Also by Diana Delacruz

God always has a purpose. We always have a choice.

In this compelling Genesis Award finalist, fifteen-year-old Melissa Travis finds herself floundering into uncharted waters when she is exiled from her Christian high school. Dreading a month of "mom talks" over endless cups of tea, she accepts her missionary sister's invitation to visit the remote Chiloé Islands of southern Chile. There she discovers a world utterly unlike the South Pacific paradise she imagined, where dire poverty dwells with enchanting beauty, and ancient customs conspire with modern corruption. While a pod of playful dolphins casts an irresistible spell, sinister evil simmers beneath the surface.

A suspicious drowning, a ghost ship, and a shaman's chilling prediction of her death on the island force Melissa to question everything she believes. Amid the storm of human greed and natural disasters, a soulful young islander inspires her to make life-changing choices, while faith and friendship draw her to reckon with destiny.